# MARGIN FOR ERROR

*A Satirical Melodrama*

*by*

## CLARE BOOTHE

*with an introduction by*

### HENRY R. LUCE

**RANDOM HOUSE**
**NEW YORK**

*Photograph by Vandamm*

*For*
DR. RUDOLF KOMMER
AND
DR. MILTON ROSENBLÜTH
WITH AFFECTION
THIS SMALL FOOTNOTE ON
A GIGANTIC QUESTION

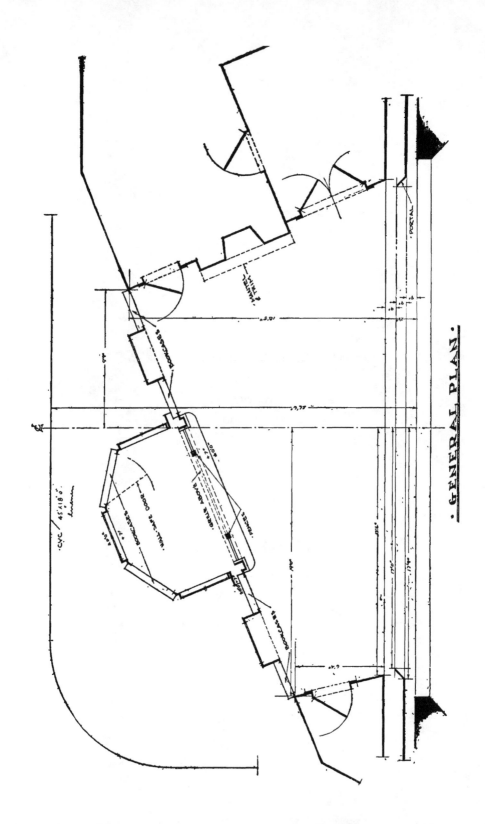

· GENERAL PLAN ·

# INTRODUCTION

*By* Henry R. Luce

In Clare Boothe's *Margin for Error,* the Great Reich's highest diplomatic representative in New York City, the duly accredited, duly recognized representative of 80,000,000 of the most competent inhabitants of the globe, is poisoned, stabbed, shot. The play opened, to smart audiences in Washington and New York, just as the Great German Reich was completing on the plains of Poland the most masterly exhibition of triumphant terror in the long history of war. The Leader of the Great German Reich, having exhibited to a vast and fascinated audience in the Americas and elsewhere as much of that spectacle as he desired, was now drawing across it the curtain of blackest censorship while he announced from the rostrum of the German Parliament that far more terrible terror would descend upon all who might ever thereafter oppose the Great German Reich. Every man and woman in the Washington and New York theaters knew that Adolf Hitler had already been given his answer. Every man and woman had heard George VI, speaking to his people, say:

> "In this grave hour, perhaps the most fateful in our history, I send to every household of my peoples, both at home and overseas, this message, spoken with the same depths of feeling for each one of you as if I were able to cross your thresholds and speak to you myself. . . . We are at war."

# INTRODUCTION

Every man and woman sitting in those Washington and New York theaters had heard the King draw a deep breath and go on:

> "We have been forced into a conflict, for we are called, with our allies, to meet the challenge of a principle which, if it were to prevail, would be fatal to any civilized order in the world. . . .
>
> "This is the ultimate issue. . . . It is to this high purpose that I now call my people at home and my peoples across the seas who will make our cause their own. . . .
>
> "The task will be hard. . . . If one and all we keep resolutely faithful to it, ready for whatever service or sacrifice it may demand, then with God's help we shall prevail. May He bless and keep us all."

The play was a success. The critics reported to their publics that at last a play dealing with the National Socialist Revolution was a hit on Broadway. Bursting with anti-Nazi zeal, Walter Winchell proclaimed himself Miss Boothe's Press Agent No. 1. With ecstatic sincerity he urged: "Go and enjoy hearing her players speak their minds for you in these hateful times abroad." John Anderson described the thrice-murdered German Consul General as the "most satisfying likeness of official German ferocity that we have yet had on the stage." At Washington, the German Embassy muttered something about protest and the acclaim of the first successful anti-Nazi play continued. A syndicated article on the theater under banner headlines began:

> "Next to the British blockade . . . the cause of the Nazi Reich has not sustained as great a disaster as Clare Boothe's new play . . . launched at the Plymouth Theatre to the huzzahs and plaudits of a highly enthusiastic initial audience. Reams of singeing editorials . . . and hundreds

of sulphuric condemnations of Nazi behavior over the air will not have as much effect as this one play. . . ."

Although, to be sure, very few people were moved to any such flamboyant hyperbole as the above—nevertheless *Margin for Error* has, I think, an importance outside and beyond the theater. Its importance does not arise from the fact that it at last clarified a surging, turgid rush of American emotion in the World Crisis and, having given a name to action, made action possible—for it did no such thing. Its importance lies in exactly the opposite direction. For it demonstrated that Americans were afraid—afraid to think. Americans were afraid of the kind of thinking where thought is fused with emotion—the only kind of thinking which leads to conclusions and to action. Some people walked out of this play angrily saying, for anyone to hear, "Dirty propaganda." But most people liked it—because, with its satire and wit and humor and gaily exaggerated melodrama, it deflected them (and hence protected them) from having to come to conclusions.

At about the time of this play's performance, *McCall's Magazine* was conducting a Forum for Youth. This is what one youth said:

"Well, I've been thinking right here. . . . I've been sitting here racking my brains to see whether there's anything at all I thought about, definitely and positively, and really, I've no faith in anything. I'm getting afraid to think, because I fear I may get emotional about it."

The critics one and all applauded Miss Boothe for at last having found the way to deal with the National Socialist Revolution. The way to deal with it was to ridicule it. Mr. Anderson took pleasure in reminding Miss Boothe that a year previously he had publicly wished that Miss Boothe might bend her talents to something worthy of them and had in fact suggested that her satire was just the thing to train on Adolf. Other critics less foresighted or less solicitous for Miss Boothe's talent were at great pains to point out exactly why it was that nothing could be said seriously on the stage about the long-maturing and now erupted Crisis and why therefore, and by what canons of what art, it was inevitably the satirist who alone should succeed in getting National Socialism on stage. But some of the critics went even further. Not content with excusing the theater for its inability to compete, straight on, with headlines, some of them went on to display the ultimate loyalty to the Art they serve by announcing that since National Socialism had succumbed to Satire on the stage, so also must National Socialism succumb to Satire in life. Sidney Whipple, one of the most genial of critics, finds, for example, that "Miss Boothe treats the entire ideology of the Reich Government as something which, when the world's sense of humor is at last restored, will be laughed to death." Since Miss Boothe nowhere makes this prediction explicit, I think it is fair to ascribe this idea to Mr. Whipple himself. But regardless of who should get credit for the idea, it is an analysis of the World Crisis which, if correct, might obviously save the British Empire the loss of so much blood and treasure that no time should be lost in transmitting it to Mr. Winston Churchill—in exchange for immediate payment of the last war debt.

And will there also be established here a League for the Restoration of the World's Sense of Humor? For it is not for Europeans that we agitate ourselves; it is our own skins, if we are to believe certain other critics, which were saved by Miss Boothe's salutary sense of humor. Thus, in the nation's capital, Nelson Bell of the *Washington Post* reported: "*Margin for Error* accomplishes its purpose of laying the twisted thinking and warped political ideology of Berlin in the dust-bin both by riddling, direct fire and a smothering barrage of ridicule. There is not much left for America to fear by the time the final curtain descends upon the second and last act."

It is, of course, my contention that America has just about everything to fear which the most powerful nation in the world can possibly fear, as long as it is content to weigh Hitler in the balance and find him unequal to a jest.

This preference for a jest, this seeing satire as the only weapon to fight National Socialism—as borne out by the public's relish of *Margin for Error*—proved as clearly as any event in 1939 that the American people either did not dare to say what they meant, or did not wish to have what they said mean anything. It proved not that the American people were honestly confused (for as the self-admittedly best-informed people in history they knew what it was all about) but that they *desired* to be confused, were at great pains to confuse themselves, applauded the confusion, hoped they might painlessly confuse themselves right straight through World War II, and wake up in a fine mood of clarity on some happy summer's day with nothing worse to worry about than the birds twittering too far in advance of the 8:10 Commuter's Special. In short, *Margin for Error* indicated that the United States of America was advancing into its own Munich—a zigzag isolationist course from which it may or may not extricate itself with honor and success.

Turning now to a consideration of the play itself, the outstanding fact is that *Margin for Error* is the first successful play about the National Socialist Revolution. Probably 80 per cent of all U. S. playwrights had wrestled with the problem. All credit to those who produced *something*. Messrs. Kaufman and Hart, able and patriotic, offered *The American Way* (*circa* 1895-1939), but their attack on Nazism had no sooner developed a fine momentum than it broke down somewhere about the year 1910. Other playwrights were strangely silent. It might have been expected, for example, that Lillian Hellman, who combines Messianic political views with a professional specialization in sadism, would have produced a nice anti-Nazi item. Actually she got no nearer to the World Crisis than a rich Louisianian's lust for killing rabbits—also in approximately the year 1910—or was it only 1900? What Philip Barry might have been thinking, theatrically, about Nazism it is difficult to imagine, once it is admitted that the whole subject is in bad taste and of little interest to a God Who takes a liberal view of adultery. In *No Time for Comedy* Sam Behrman did produce some excellent conversation on the subject which might have been better appreciated had not both critics and audience been currently so confused by the then trouble in Spain. There has indeed been one really fine anti-Nazi play—Robert Sherwood's *Abe Lincoln in Illinois*. But that, of course, did not involve the problem of getting the National Socialist Revolution in action and reaction on stage.

Where all others have so far failed, Miss Boothe has half-succeeded. But her peculiar success does not really lie in having got National Socialism on stage. Her success—or rather what will later be defined as her half-success—is her success in dramatizing the democrat's rebuttal to National Socialism. For in all these years of failure the difficulty has not in fact been to get National Socialism on stage. The real difficulty has been to get on stage a convincing *rebuttal* to

National Socialism. It is in this that Miss Boothe has half-succeeded. She succeeded with her character Moe Finkelstein, the Jewish policeman. Her success is glorious, a heart-warming triumph. She failed with Thomas S. Denny, the just-an-American. Her failure is a dull thump—a failure of some significance because symptomatic of a failure in contemporary American life.

The critics have almost unanimously absolved the theater and the playwrights for the failure to produce any adequate plays concerning National Socialism. They have all put forth the same excuse. They have all said that the real facts about National Socialism are so terrific that not even the most inspired make-believe could possibly achieve emotional validity. But surely in all this the critics have been strangely forgetful. They have forgotten that all the theater is ever expected to do is put individual characters on stage—and that it has achieved its many triumphs through the ages by putting characters on stage. If Harriet Beecher Stowe got Negro slavery on stage, she did it by inventing Simon Legree—and Uncle Tom. In *Lysistrata,* Aristophanes wrote against war by creating women who refused to sleep with their husbands as long as they remained warriors.

So the question is begged by the critics if they say it is impossible to get National Socialism on stage in the shape of one or two or a dozen dramatically convincing individual Nazis. The answer is that it is not impossible. The answer is that it has been done. Powerful individual Nazis have been got on stage, and not only by Miss Boothe and not only in satire. The real difficulty—and this is the point where I think the critics have gone awry in their analyses—the difficulty has been to get on stage the rebuttal to National Socialism; that is to say, the difficulty has been to create a believable democrat. Many characters have been created who convincingly reflect an environment of Brutality, Dictatorship, Regimentation and Untruth. But few characters have been created who adequately reflect an environment of Freedom and Kindness and Justice and Truth—an environment, at the very least, of faith in the public and private virtues.

In *Till the Day I Die,* Clifford Odets was fully successful in convincing his audience of the frightful brutality inherent in Nazism. But he offered no rebuttal. You were supposed to offer your own rebuttal. And what was your rebuttal supposed to be? What except to say, with a shudder, "I don't like brutality"? Mr. Odets' theater no doubt offered a valuable catharsis for the brutality in all of us. But while his brutality was convincing, it contributed nothing to an understanding either of the nature of brutality or of the means or faith by which men may overcome brutality. Mr. Odets staged convincing crucifixions, but his crucifixions had no power to save. There were no Christs on his barricades. There was no redemption in the blood he spilled.

Of the other anti-Nazi plays which failed, almost all deserved to fail; but not because they did not create plausible Nazis. Such plays as *Waltz in Goose Step, Lorelei, The Brown Danube* failed because they were not interesting enough theater, or were not powerful enough propaganda, or were *unintentionally* melodramatic while striving to be deeply thoughtful. In one of them—*Lorelei*—the thinking was muddled; in more than one the writing was mediocre. But in almost all of them the Nazi characters were credible.

Now similarly Miss Boothe has done well enough in getting National Socialism convincingly on stage in the person of thrice-murdered German Consul General Baumer and of his secretary, Baron von Alvenstor. Personally, I am not so enthusiastic about the character of the Consul. I do not agree with Mr. Anderson that he is the "most satisfying likeness of official German ferocity that we have yet had on the stage." He inevitably suffers from having to satisfy the requirements of a murder melodrama. If National Socialism is nothing more than Otto L. Preminger, we would indeed have nothing to fear. If Mr. H. R. Knickerbocker's famous scoop about the top Nazis having all cached millions of dollars abroad is true—then the British Empire has nothing to fear. The British Empire, having always honored its bank depositors, can undoubtedly provide for any number of retired Nazi leaders any number of pleasant, green-lawned estates at fair prices and with the equal protection of England's justly famous laws. No, Herr Baumer neither terrifies nor pleases me particularly as a character beyond his usefulness for melodrama. A far sounder achievement, it seems to me, is Miss Boothe's invention of Baron von Alvenstor. He commands my respect, even my liking—and it is a man like the Baron who could really terrify me. It happens in the play, and quite usefully for the plot, that the Baron's grandmother is a Jewess and he is thereby fortuitously un-Nazified. This un-Nazification of a Nazi is beautifully handled. But just suppose the Baron's grandmother hadn't been a Jewess, or had never been discovered—then you would have had in the Baron a really terrifying character. A man of intelligence, efficient, well-integrated, a lover of music (and thereby immune from Shakespeare's criterion for scoundrelism) who is eagerly willing to live and work and die for all the things which are the exact opposite of all the things which Americans have been taught are most worth living and working and dying for. And since his faith and devotion seem obviously so much greater than the faith and devotion which we democrats see about us, he would become for us a profoundly important and provocative character.

The difficulty, then, is not with the antagonists of Freedom, but with its champions. And here is where Miss Boothe has won her really famous victory. For the character of Moe Finkelstein is the best advertisement of Democracy since Sherwood's *Lincoln*. Here is a citizen and servant of the biggest and most complicated metropolis on earth. Here is also the citizen of a Republic. And neither circumstance has got him down. On the contrary he loves life. He is full of bounce and vigor and enthusiasm. He is proud and happy in his service to his city. He is well disciplined. He adores his Jewish mamma. He has a beautiful and cheerful way with a pretty and available woman. And—there is no doubt whatever there are things he will die for and, little though he understands "ideology," he knows pretty well what those things are. There is little doubt that he would gladly die in defense of the Republic of the United States. There is little doubt that, if he were told by superiors he respected such as Mulrooney or the Mayor that the defense of Liberty and Justice throughout the world somehow impinged on him, he would gladly go into any hell they told him to go into.

But, for him, these issues are not joined during his busy evening at the Plymouth Theatre. The issue he does meet is quite enough for one young fellow in one evening—and he meets it nobly. He has to decide, and decide in a split second, whether to play safe for himself, or whether to take great personal risk in order to avert possible harm to a lot of un-

American people overseas. No one prompts him. It is he who sees the issue—sees it in a flash and makes his decision instantly—on the side of the angels and of personal sacrifice. I am a better and happier citizen of the Republic for having encountered Moe Finkelstein.

There is nothing wrong with Moe Finkelstein. But there is something very wrong with Thomas Denny, the just-an-American. The trouble with Thomas Denny is that he doesn't exist. Not that he is dead—he will never die because he never lived. Thomas Denny is a fine, good-looking lump of stale dough which, when squeezed by the author, produces mechanical sound effects. And for having trailed him around the theater for a whole evening, I am a worse and sadder citizen of this Republic. And I couldn't help trailing him because he, if anyone on stage, was intended to represent me— and you, dear reader. For he was you and I as "just-American," without any special personal point of contact with Adolf Hitler because we don't happen to be Jews and we don't happen at the moment to be mixed up in business dealings with or against the Reich—and you and I don't even happen to have just fallen in love with a beautiful Czech whose father Mr. Hitler is about to fry. We and Thomas Denny (apart from his doubtful romance) are just Americans who listen day after day and month after month to Mr. Hitler telling us that Democracy is a putrid disease, that the German Reich is going to conquer now this and now that part of the world, in short as much as it chooses to, that treaties are made to be broken, that International Law is a lot of tommyrot, that Jews are disgusting swine and may properly be persecuted, that Czechs are disgusting swine and may properly be persecuted, that Slavs are disgusting swine and may properly be persecuted, that Poles are disgusting swine and may properly be persecuted, that whoever Hitler says are disgusting swine are therefore disgusting swine and may properly be persecuted; that lies and terrorism are perfectly proper instruments of statecraft; that Christianity is largely nonsense, and is to be tolerated only as it submits itself to the Third Reich and only at the pleasure of the Third Reich; that the Third Reich is to be the sole judge of scientific truth; that the Third Reich shall determine just what works of art in any field shall be produced and what shall not be produced; finally that individuals are of no importance and have no rights; that individuals—meaning you and me—are simply chattels of something called the State and that he will tell us from time to time, subject to change without notice, whether he approves of the State to which you and I belong or whether it will suit his convenience to destroy it; that whether or not he destroys you and me in the process of destroying any particular State is a matter of utter indifference to him; and telling us all this day after day, month after month, he asks what are you going to do about it? And he also teaches us, you and me, the answer. Answer: Nothing, dear teacher.

Certainly Thomas Denny has nothing to say—nothing except the tritest and stalest platitudes, and the play seems to come to an embarrassing full stop whenever he is required to open his mouth. And obviously he is required both to be there and to speak, for surely, even in a satirical melodrama, the defense of Democracy ought not to be left to the unsupported efforts of one Jewish policeman.

Miss Boothe may have intended some slight compliment to my profession when she chose a journalist to represent the invisible supporting cast of 130,000,000 Americans. But obviously Miss Boothe cared so little about this hulking newspaper man that she never stopped to consider what he might be thinking about during the hours in which it never occurs to him to telephone to his paper the biggest murder scoop of the year. A bad newspaper man, an unconvincing lover and a stale democrat—the measure of frustration is complete.

In *Margin for Error* Thomas Denny is only a minor character. But apropos of Thomas Denny I say that the real problem of dealing theatrically with the National Socialist Revolution has not been met. For Thomas Denny is not a believable democrat—he is not much of a believable anything. I applaud *Margin for Error*, but as a long and faithful customer of the theater, I am still waiting hungrily for the theater to give me a believable, disinterested democrat. In the face of a worldwide challenge to all that we have ever felt about Liberty and Justice and Truth, let us see a man, without any particular ax to grind, and not so very much better than any of us, who will throw back in the face of that challenge an enthusiastic love of Freedom, championing of Truth and defense of Justice.

But perhaps before that happens the believable democrat will have to create himself—in the cities and villages, in the factories and farms, of this Republic. And more especially in the timorous schools and colleges, in the scared and inward-looking executive offices of industry and commerce—and in the needlessly confused sanctums of editors and broadcasters and spiritual pastors. The materials for this re-creation lie all about us and within us—all that we cherish most in our inheritance from the past, all our deepest hopes for the future, everything which, by the grace of God, gives dignity to human life. I, for one, have not the slightest doubt that this great drama of re-creation will occur, is indeed already occurring. The dramatist who can vitalize this occurrence will have justified in himself all that has ever been claimed for a free art in a land of freedom. That dramatist, I regret to say, is not, at the moment, my dear wife, Miss Boothe.

*Greenwich, Conn.*
*January 31, 1940.*

*Margin for Error* was produced by Richard Aldrich and Richard Myers at the Plymouth Theatre, New York City, on November 3, 1939, with the following cast:

| | |
|---|---|
| OTTO B. HORST | Philip Coolidge |
| BARON MAX VON ALVENSTOR | Bramwell Fletcher |
| OFFICER MOE FINKELSTEIN | Sam Levene |
| FRIEDA | Evelyn Wahle |
| DR. JENNINGS | Bert Lytell |
| SOPHIE BAUMER | Elspeth Eric |
| KARL BAUMER | Otto L. Preminger |
| THOMAS S. DENNY | Leif Erickson |
| CAPTAIN MULROONEY | Edward McNamara |

*Directed by* OTTO L. PREMINGER
*Setting by* DONALD OENSLAGER

# SCENE

## ACT ONE

The Library of the German Consul in an American City, prior to September, 1939. Late afternoon.

## ACT TWO

The same.

The action of the play is continuous.

# ACT ONE

# ACT ONE

*The Consul General's library on the second floor of a house of the brownstone era.*

*This is a large room, paneled in clumsily carved stained oak. Its most prominent architectural feature is a deep-mullioned, book-lined bay window, which forms an alcove across half of the rear wall, almost a small room in itself. This bay, architecturally separated from the room by a step leading up to it and a railing on either side, can be completely cut off from the rest of the room by drawing a pair of heavy mustard-colored brocade curtains. In the bay, facing the window and just missing the curtains when drawn, is a big, square desk. Before it, looking toward the street, a high-backed leather swivel chair. When the chair is turned squarely before the desk, the right profile of the occupant would be squarely to the audience. In the wall behind the desk, a small safe, disguised as a panel of books, with its door facing the audience. Through the window one can indistinctly see a neighboring building, and a view of what might be a park.*

*On the rear wall, right and left of the bay, a pair of windows, also hung with mustard-colored drapes, with a small chair before each one. Between them and the bay, the wall spaces are paneled with books. In front of the one panel (right) a marble pedestal on which stands a bronze bust of Adolf Hitler. In front of the other panel (left) floor standards of the American flag and the Nazi flag.*

*In the left wall, center, an ornate fireplace, with a clock,*

3

*and over it a map of Germany. In front of the fireplace, and running parallel to it, a small settee, and flanking the settee, rear, close to the fireplace, a big barrel-winged armchair. Downstage next to the settee, a cabinet victrola-and-radio, behind it a high table with a telephone, which is used by* MAX *for sorting his dispatches. On the floor beside this table, a dispatch-case, sealed with swastika stickers. Downstage on this left wall, a double door, which, opened, gives a view of the hall, and another door off the hall which goes into* MAX's *office. Rear, on this wall and on the other side of the fireplace, another door, which leads directly from the library into* MAX's *office.*

*The entire right wall is also book-lined and hung with etchings of Wagnerian operas, framed newsphotos of Nazi rallies, etc. Downstage, a cellarette-bar-cabinet equipped with liquor carafes, glasses, trays on which there are several bottles of beer, soda siphons, ice containers, etc. Rear, in this right wall, a door leading to the living quarters of the Consul. Right, downstage, near this bar, and running parallel to the footlights, a sofa. To the right of it, an easy chair. Between the easy chair and the sofa, a low table.*

*The room is lit by bronze wall sconces, controlled from a switch at the double door.*

*The sconces over the flags and the bust of Hitler have been altered by the present occupant of the house into makeshift "spots," which, when turned on, throw dramatic little pools of light on the bust of Hitler and on the blood-red Nazi buntings, and tend to throw the alcove in between into deep shadow.*

*The general effect of the room with the lights off, as they are now, is one of solidity and gloom. As the afternoon wanes, the gloom deepens.*

4

# MARGIN FOR ERROR

*As the curtain rises,* OTTO HORST *is standing on the step of the alcove, center, reading a speech to* BARON MAX VON ALVENSTOR, *who sits on the sofa, his back to* HORST, *listening, smoking.* OTTO HORST, *the American Bund leader, is a fat, forty-year-old ex-elocution teacher, with a pasty intra-mural complexion, who has attempted in vain to suppress his pedagogical pudginess by wearing a tight-fitting Nazi-brown military uniform. To the same vain and martial end he has drawn and quartered his pompous carcass with a series of interlocking belts, slung with leather pouches and a knife-sheath.* HORST *is ruthless but timid, he is without a shred of humor, and is generally dour, unless drunk with his own verbosity. Always having imagined himself as a cunning fellow, he is really a facile target for any form of guile or mischief which originates in a superior mind. He is a pushover for flattery, and when it is not forthcoming from others, he is quick to knock himself practically insensible with it. 'Tis a pity he is an American. The Consul's secretary,* BARON MAX, *is a German, which is also a pity. For he is a nice fellow, a German of the spiritual stamp who sincerely believes that the Treaty of Versailles is the one great crime of history. To him the word "Kultur" really represents German poetry, philosophy and music, and not the guns, which he is nevertheless willing to see used to defend them. He is blond, blue-eyed, well bred and well tailored; in short, he is the exact opposite of all his own leaders. Having studied at Oxford, he speaks faultless English, and in his conversation with* HORST *simply cannot control an attitude of superiority and boredom.*

HORST
(*Declaiming*)

... that the American-Germanic peoples' Bunds stand for

5

peace, for jobs, for freedom. But not jobs for Communists, traitors, and war-mongers! Some say we are not American. Is it un-American to say that all Jews are Communists?

MAX
(*Coolly*)

No, but it's inaccurate.

HORST

Please, Baron! . . . And that all Jews who are not Communists are Capitalists? (OFFICER MOE FINKELSTEIN *enters quietly, closing the hall door softly behind him*) They either congregate in secret cellars, plotting to undermine law and order, or they live on the fat of the land, while the downtrodden Aryan toils!

(MOE *is in his late twenties, small, slender and almost handsome in a rather wistful Jewish way. Elaborately and awkwardly polite to his superiors, he is nevertheless fully conscious of his status as a public functionary. His demonstrations of good-will could only be mistaken by snobs for servility. In common with most of the people of his race, he has the gifts of ready sympathy, loquacity and inquisitiveness. Born in some sub-human crevice of a large American city, he has kept intact his allegiance to his family and to his God. It is the passionate conviction of his life that the nationals of all other countries are misguided and unfortunate. For the short time he stands in the door now, he watches* HORST *with calm and lofty disgust.* MAX *sees him first.*)

MAX

One minute, Horst. (*To* MOE) Yes?

6

MOE

(*Saluting*)

Officer Finkelstein, replacing Officer Kapinski on the front door from four to seven—

MAX

Oh, you're a new man—

MOE

Are you the Consul?

MAX

No, I'm Baron von Alvenstor, his secretary—

MOE

My orders is—

MAX

Please wait outside, officer. I'm busy—

MOE

Please excuse me. (*Salutes smartly, exits.*)

HORST

(*Apoplectic*)

Jewish policemen to guard this Consulate! If I were Hitler, I'd break off diplomatic relations—

MAX

Get on with it, Horst.

HORST

(*Clearing his throat*)

Um— But as long as one swastika is left in America, the Star of David will never wave over the White House! (*He*

7

*folds the speech and pockets it*) You like it? I favor short speeches. Like Abraham Lincoln.

MAX

Horst, I don't like it.

HORST

Nevertheless, my delivery is excellent. I didn't teach elocution in a Milwaukee high school twenty years for nothing. (*Smugly*) How the humble have risen.

MAX

You harp too much on the race issue.

HORST

Baron, I've analyzed our political situation thoroughly. We have no belligerent neighbors. That chops the heart out of half the totalitarian arguments—

MAX

And what about the "unequal distribution of wealth"?

HORST

Oh, the New Deal has that argument patented. Besides, nobody starves here. At least very few people—

MAX

You should make an issue of these exceptions—

HORST

*Then* how different would I sound from a Communist? No, Baron, my best bet is to create conflict among creeds and colors. Then step in, when they're exhausted, and take the

8

whole country over—*bang!* Next week I attack the Catholics, Masons, Negroes, and Café Society.

MAX

Perhaps you'd better just purge Elsa Maxwell, and leave the rest to Hitler. (*This is a dismissal*) Are your reports ready?

HORST

(*Taking a swastika-stamped envelope from a pouch at his belt*) Everything.

MAX

The dispatch leaves by airmail at midnight to catch the *Bremen.*

HORST

Lists of new memberships. Pamphlets distributed anonymously to libraries, labor halls, waiting-rooms. (*Parenthetically*) We've done very well in dentists' offices. People seem to leave them in a frame of mind for our messages. (*Slyly, as he hands* MAX *his reports*) And I've included an advance copy of the final Dies report—snitched, to use a boy's phrase, right off the Congressman's desk!

MAX

(*Bewildered*)

The Dies report?

HORST

The Congressman finds great Nazi strength everywhere. You just must send that on to Berlin! In fact, um—it's the only encouraging report we *could* send. (*Handing* MAX *another paper*) And my new budget of Bund expenses. Baron, I'm very low on funds.

9

MAX

(*Putting the reports in the safe*)
The Consul gave you ten thousand last month.

HORST

No, he didn't—

MAX

(*Surprised*)
He didn't?

HORST

No. And I must have the money to pay for these new uniforms.

MAX

Who told you to buy new uniforms?

HORST

I've got to do *something* to get my picture in the papers!
Short of fan dancers or murder, nothing seems to astonish the
American public.

MAX

You always bank carefully?

HORST

Under twenty different names in twenty different banks.
"Cautious Otto," you could call me.

MAX

(*Disgusted*)
"Cautious Otto"? That wouldn't sound any better in the
papers than "The Milwaukee Schoolmaster."

**HORST**

Oh, I'm joking. Cautious! Just to be the American Fuehrer is the height of recklessness. (*Opens hall door.* MOE *is seen standing stiffly outside*) Well, I'll be back after the rally for the money. (*Clapping on his hat, and saluting with ludicrous enthusiasm*) Heil Hitler! . . . You can go in now, Officer Finkelstein. (*Exits as* MOE *enters.*)

**MAX**

Now, Officer. You know your duties?

**MOE**

Positively.

**MAX**

The door to the left goes into my office—

**MOE**

Yeah, and the reception room is opposite. I got the whole layout.

**MAX**

Chancellor Hitler broadcasts at 5 o'clock.

**MOE**

I know all the angles. With Finkelstein and Solomon on duty, there ain't gonna be no ruckus on this block—God forbid! (*Raps the nearest piece of wood.*)

**MAX**

(*Smiling*)

Then that's all, thank you. I'll tell the Consul you've reported.

MOE

(*Uneasily*)

The boys say he kinda likes to conduct his own initiation.

MAX

Officer, you won't find the Consul difficult, if you don't antagonize him.

MOE

I don't antagonize anybody that ain't askin' for it. (*Coming a little closer to* MAX, *and with genuine curiosity*) Are *you* a Nazi?

MAX

Naturally.

MOE

(*Shrugging*)

What's so naturally about it? (MAX's *smile disappears*) Pardon me. I'm too conversational. But I'd like to give you a steer about this Otto Horst. Can him! He's earmarked for the pen.

MAX

(*Curious*)

Why?

MOE

He don't even know how to run his own racket. Which is softer than most rackets. (*Disgusted*) He can wrap himself up in an American flag to run it.

MAX

Free speech is part of *your* Constitution.

MOE

Yeah. But when a guy like Otto stands on his Constitutional rights to preach murder—there oughta be some Constitutional way to give *him* a military funeral!

MAX

(*Coldly*)

That will do, Officer.

MOE

O.K. (*Going to door*) But I'm telling you—Das Otto is headed for der Clink. You just wanna look out, when his time comes you don't get mugged and finger-printed with him. But why should I tip you guys off? I'm too democratic. (*Suddenly turning*) Oh . . . !

MAX

Now what?

MOE

Did somebody die in this house this morning?

MAX

Certainly not.

MOE

Well, Officer Solomon says your German maid wouldn't give him no cup of coffee today, on account she was sore that a Mr. Churchill kicked off here this morning. I guess Sol don't talk such good German—

MAX

Oh, Mr. Churchill? Yes, he died here.

13

MOE

(*Professionally truculent*)

Say, anybody dies on the premises, you gotta report it—

MAX

Mr. Churchill was a parrot.

MOE

A parrot?

MAX

Yes, Winston Churchill, Mrs. Baumer's pet parrot. He was poisoned.

MOE

How'd that take place?

MAX

At breakfast. Herr Baumer received a box of grapes from an anonymous admirer. He gave . . . (*quickly*) Well, the parrot got hold of them. . . .

MOE

(*Wistfully*)

Lucky it wasn't Mr. Baumer?

MAX

Very.

MOE

Now was that so smart? To sit at table with a bunch of anomynous fruit?

MAX

Perhaps not.

14

MOE

A guy like the Consul which ain't exactly popular oughta watch his diet.

MAX

We are *all* very careful, Officer.

MOE

(*Cheerfully*)

Well, nice pleasant home life you got here. (*Enter* FRIEDA) Please excuse me.

> (FRIEDA *is a well-cushioned, trim little blonde. Her whole appearance is a testimonial that the husband of the house is master here. Only a powerless or indifferent wife would engage such a maid.* MOE *beams at her with honest admiration as he steps back from the door to let her come in.*)

FRIEDA

(*Ignoring* MOE *rather ostentatiously*)

Herr Baron, Dr. Jennings ist hier. Wollen Sie ihm empfangen?

MAX

Ja, Frieda.

FRIEDA

(*Distorting her pretty face into a grimace of. hate, as she passes* MOE)

Niederträchtiger Judischer Giftmischer! (*Exits.*)

MOE

(*Laughing, to* MAX)

Well, that was a fast brush-off. Please excuse me. (*He exits as* DR. JENNINGS *enters.* DR. JENNINGS *is a fine-looking, middle-*

*aged practitioner who generally carries his well-bred, gentle but efficient bedside manner into all the activities of his daily life. At the moment, however, it is apparent that his usual self-confidence has deserted him. He is agitated and is controlling himself with difficulty.*)

DR. JENNINGS

Good afternoon, Baron.

MAX

Good afternoon, Dr. Jennings. . . .

DR. JENNINGS

I happened to be making a call in the neighborhood. Has any news come for me on the *Bremen?*

MAX

The Consul is not home yet. The dispatch hasn't been sorted. (*He points to the unopened dispatch box on his desk, then turns to the doctor, and half-bows him toward the door*) I'll telephone you later, Doctor.

DR. JENNINGS

Baron! I've been coming here for six months. I don't intend to waste any more time or money. (*Taking a folded-back newspaper out of his pocket with a trembling hand*) Have you seen Thomas Denny's column?

MAX

(*Putting the newspaper on the low table without looking at it*)

Yes, but—

16

**DR. JENNINGS**

I've followed Denny's column for a long time. He's unusually accurate. He says this Consulate is running a racket—

**MAX**

(*Honestly*)

Doctor, please believe me, Herr Baumer's made a *sincere* effort to get your friends out of Germany—

**DR. JENNINGS**

But he *must* know by this time whether or not it's hopeless! I've heard nothing from Professor Norberg and his wife in weeks—

**MAX**

The Norbergs are now in Concentration Camp 39. That means their release is imminent—

**DR. JENNINGS**

Baron, it's unthinkable that a German citizen as useful as Professor Norberg has been held for two years in a concentration camp because of lecture notes found in his scrap basket!

**MAX**

In Germany, Doctor, political lectures are dangerous.

**DR. JENNINGS**

But the man wasn't a politician—he was a scientist. He merely quoted another Aryan, Professor Earnest Hooton of Harvard: that the Jews are a biologically sound and superior race, because persecution has bred out their physical and mental weaklings.

17

MAX

Yes, but what did he say about our Fuehrer?

DR. JENNINGS

(*Walking directly to the bust of Hitler*)

All he said was that your Fuehrer is the victim of an aggravated psycho-neurosis—with obsessional paranoid trends and delusions of grandeur!

MAX

!!!

DR. JENNINGS

And as a medical man, I find the opinion conservative. (*Goes to door*) I have a call to make. I'll be back in an hour—

MAX

(*Wearily*)

Doctor, the Fuehrer is broadcasting at five. The Consul has canceled all appointments—

DR. JENNINGS

Then I will be back at 4:30. (*Firmly*) It'll be my last visit. I want a definite answer about Professor Norberg, or I'll take up this whole matter with the State Department in Washington. Good afternoon, Baron.

MAX

Good afternoon, Doctor.

> (DR. JENNINGS *exits, as the door, right, opens and* SOPHIE, *who has plainly been listening outside of it, enters.* SOPHIE *is a dark, pretty, vaguely foreign-looking woman in her early thirties. Her brown troubled*

*eyes emphasize the dramatic pallor of her face. She
speaks English with the attractive precision of a
woman who has several languages at the command
of her moods. She is dressed for the street.*)

SOPHIE

That was Dr. Jennings?

MAX

Yes.

SOPHIE

I couldn't bear to face him. (*Bitterly*) Max, it's disgraceful—

MAX

Karl really has tried to help him—

SOPHIE

All right. (*Tugging on her gloves and going to the window*)
But what about all those other poor people who come here?
He hasn't really tried to help them. He takes their money,
and never even writes a word to Berlin about their relatives.

MAX

How do you know he takes money?

SOPHIE

He doesn't let them come here because he feels sorry for
them. . . . (*Looking eagerly into the street*) What time is it?

MAX

It's almost four o'clock.

19

SOPHIE

When Karl comes in, tell him I've gone shopping—

MAX

You'll miss Hitler's speech.

SOPHIE

I don't want to hear Hitler's speech. They're all alike. The only novelty it could have for me would be if somebody shot him in the middle of it. (*She goes to door, left.*)

MAX
(*Gently*)

Sophie . . . (*She pauses*) I'm awfully sorry about your parrot.

SOPHIE

Yes, it was so unnecessary.

MAX

It was rather.

SOPHIE
(*Mocking*)

It was "rather"?

MAX

What do you want me to say? That your husband deliberately poisoned the parrot?

SOPHIE
(*Softly*)

Say what you think, Max.

20

MAX

He was very angry about—Tom Denny's column!

SOPHIE

Well, it's all true, isn't it?

MAX

I don't really know. And neither do you, Sophie.

SOPHIE

You're always so loyal to him.

MAX

I'm not loyal to him. I'm loyal to what he represents—

SOPHIE

(*Disgusted*)

The Nazis.

MAX

Yes. The Nazis. (*Coldly*) Sophie, *you* gave that story to Tom Denny for his paper—

SOPHIE

(*Frightened*)

No, Max!

MAX

Yes. And you also gave him the story last week that Otto Horst reports directly here for Berlin orders. Sophie, I know how you feel about Germany now, but it's got to stop! (*Gently*) You know I am very fond of you—

SOPHIE
(*Reassured*)

I know that—

MAX

But if there's going to be any conflict between my friendship and my duty—

SOPHIE

Of course, Max! (*Frightened again*) Does Karl know I told Tom Denny?

MAX

I hope not!

SOPHIE

Max, thank you for warning me. It is—just a warning?

MAX

That's all. (*Patting her hand*) Now forget it.

SOPHIE
(*Rebellious*)

But why is it patriotism when you and Karl spy on America —and treason when I spy on Germany?

MAX

You're a German citizen—

SOPHIE

No! My father's a Czech. My mother was an American—

MAX

You're still the Consul's wife.

22

SOPHIE

I don't want to be any longer! But he won't give me a divorce. (*In despair*) Oh, Max, what am I going to do?

MAX

Why don't you leave him?

SOPHIE

My father is still . . . in Prague, Max.

MAX
(*Smiling*)
Oh, Karl wouldn't take it out on your father.

SOPHIE

You're so sensitive about most people. But you really don't know Karl, do you?

MAX

He hasn't had an easy job in this post. He has plenty to worry about. I quite understand how *you* feel, but my relation to him is different. He's my chief. (*Uneasily*) I've got to give him the benefit of every doubt— (*There is a heavy step in the hall, and a loud, angry voice.*)

CONSUL
(*Off stage, to* FRIEDA)
Warum öffnen sie die türe nicht schneller?

FRIEDA

Entschuldigen Sie, Herr Konsul—
(SOPHIE, *caught, retreats to the door, right.*)

23

SOPHIE

(*To* MAX, *whispering*)

You haven't seen me. . . . (*Exits a split second before the* CONSUL *enters.*)

(CONSUL KARL BAUMER *is the type of German who makes caricaturists' lives easy, and pro-German propaganda difficult. He is a type, moreover, by no means uncommon in official Germany. He has a completely shaven, glistening bullet head, he is tough, pallid and fleshy, though despite his flabby awkwardness, he can move, when the occasion requires, with alarming alacrity. In quiescent moments his eyes are remarkable for an expression of gentle and bovine torpor, which is, of course, a carefully fostered piece of deception. A born sycophant, he is therefore unrelentingly arrogant to his dependents. Something of a sadist, and a good deal of a glutton, he fancies himself as a bon-vivant and man of the world. He wears a bat-wing collar, pin-stripe morning trousers and a monocle. These archaic elegances do little to soften his definitely prehistoric personality. He is carrying a folder of phonograph records.*)

MAX

Afternoon, sir—

CONSUL

Has the Berlin dispatch come?

MAX

Yes, sir. (*He puts the dispatch-box on the high table. The* CONSUL *hands him the key from his watch chain.* MAX *breaks the swastika seal. During the following scene* MAX *goes about the business of sorting the box's contents.*)

CONSUL

Where's Sophie?

MAX

She said she was going out.

CONSUL

I bought a new Wagner record. Liebestod. I want her to hear it. (*Puts the records by the victrola.*)

MAX

Otto Horst will be coming here after the rally for money.

CONSUL

I gave him ten thousand last month.

MAX

He says you didn't.
(*A pause.*)

CONSUL

That's right. I *did* put it off until I see his new budget. Max, how could Berlin have chosen this Dummkopf for our American Fuehrer!

MAX

(*Smiling*)

You remember the confusion in Berlin, while Goering was having that baby?

CONSUL

I have a feeling that Berlin will soon want Horst liquidated.

25

Liquidated . . . What a shame Stalin, and not Hitler, invented a beautiful word like that.

MAX

Thomas Denny predicts they will soon share it.

CONSUL

That's possible.

MAX

A Communist-Nazi Alliance?

CONSUL

Why not? Hitler could bring out a new edition of *Mein Kampf*—for one hundred and eighty million new customers. *If* he could collect the rubles.

MAX

Well, if that day ever comes, I cease to be a Nazi.

CONSUL

(*Fixing his monocle cynically*)
You're so sure of everything, Max.

MAX

(*Heatedly*)
I am sure of that, sir, or I haven't understood my Fuehrer.

CONSUL

Let's hope nobody understands him. Peace is a static state of misunderstanding. When nations understand each other clearly, war is inevitable.

MAX

That's too cynical a philosophy for me, sir. . . . Horst likes
his job. He wouldn't be so easy to liquidate.

CONSUL

(*Plumping himself into the easy chair*)
Still, a nice little plan is working in me.

MAX

Another of your inspirations?

CONSUL

Yes. My inspirations come to me as they come to Hitler—
(*Taps his brow, with unconscious humor*) out of nothing.

MAX

(*Smiling*)
When you get your inspiration, do give me an inkling.

CONSUL

(*With lightly ironic emphasis*)
Max, sometimes you are too *curious.*

MAX

I've never thought of myself as unduly curious—

CONSUL

Perhaps it is an *English* trait.

MAX

So far as I know, I inherited nothing from my English
grandmother.

CONSUL

How can we know what we inherit from our grandparents, if we know so little about them . . . as in *your* case?

MAX

After all, my grandfather was a Prussian nobleman—

CONSUL

Don't apologize, Baron. We Nazis are not class conscious—

MAX

I mean, my grandmother was the daughter of a common English green-grocer—

CONSUL

(*Stung*)

Please remember, *I* was a common chemist, before Hitler called me.

MAX

I was only trying to explain, sir—my grandfather's generation was class conscious—and my grandmother's background— (*Deprecating his own implied snobbishness with a self-conscious laugh*) Well, they tried to forget that—

CONSUL

(*Very evenly*)

Ja. All one remembers in Berlin now is that she brought a lot of money into your family.

MAX

(*Annoyed*)

She was also very beautiful!

28

CONSUL
(*Casual to a point*)
Have you any pictures of her?

MAX
Pictures? A fellow doesn't go about carrying pictures of
his grandmother!

CONSUL
(*Softly*)
They do, quite often these days, in Germany.

MAX
Look here, sir. What are you driving at? (*He walks angrily
toward the* CONSUL, *carrying his sheaf of now-sorted papers.*)

CONSUL
(*Gently*)
Max, *why* are you so touchy?

MAX
I'm sorry . . . I've been on edge all day. I guess it was
the parrot.

CONSUL
(*Dropping all pretense of amiability*)
I am sent poisoned grapes in the mail. I suspect this smell
of bitter almonds comes from cyanide of potassium. Am I
to try it on *myself?*

MAX
You could have sent it for analysis.

CONSUL
I am daily threatened to be shot at in the street. What

29

stands between me and death? (*Waving toward the street*) *Two Jewish policemen!* You are on edge, Max. *I* am on a precipice.

MAX

You're quite right, sir. These days are beginning to tell on all of us. (*Now hands the* CONSUL *papers, one by one*) The weekly memo for you, in code. It *is* very short.

CONSUL

(*Grimacing*)

I don't like the short ones. Decode it. Anything about Professor Norberg yet?

MAX

(*Smiling*)

Yes! There's a memo— (*Reading*) "Professor Norberg has been released from Concentration Camp 39—"

CONSUL

(*Rising*)

Good. Now we can dispose of our Dr. Jennings. He was getting on my nerves.

MAX

Dr. Jennings is coming at 4:30. I couldn't put him off.

CONSUL

Good. I will see him.

MAX

(*Reading*)

I say! "Norberg's in a hospital at Dusseldorf. His wife died in the concentration camp—in childbirth. . . ."

30

CONSUL

That's terrible. (*Dismisses that paper*) Anything else?

MAX

Sir, I rather like the old doctor. This is bad news for him.
Let me tell him—

CONSUL

I said *I* will see him. Anything else?

MAX

(*Showing a big package of bills*)
The money. Fifty thousand dollars.

CONSUL

Fifty thousand—! (*Pacing, horribly irritated*) What am I
to do with fifty thousand!? Start a hundred more camps! Get
a broadcasting station! Buy up American journalists! Next
Berlin will order me to corrupt Dorothy Thompson with an
autographed picture of Hitler. (*Grabs newspaper from low
table*) I can't get even one good word from this second-rate
columnist, Thomas Denny.

MAX

(*Appalled*)
You didn't make *him* an offer?

CONSUL

Max, am I a Dummkopf? I opened the doors of this Consulate—I offered him my friendship. I answered all his im-
pertinent questions. I even let him make love to my wife!

MAX
(*Nervously*)
I say, you *are* imagining things—

CONSUL
There are certain precise facts in Mr. Denny's column—
(*Viciously*) Haven't *you* noticed?

MAX
Of course I have. But you can't accuse Sophie—

CONSUL
Now go decode that report, put the money in the safe, and
stop gossiping about my wife!

MAX
Well, that's the limit! (*He goes to safe abruptly, controlling,
no doubt, an impulse to sock his superior on the jaw.*)

CONSUL
Exactly! And my patience is exhausted.

MAX
(*Coldly*)
So is mine, sir. (*Returning from the safe where he has de-
posited the money*) Now, let's be frank. I do feel, lately, that
you doubt—my loyalty.

CONSUL
(*Unctuously*)
If I doubt your loyalty, perhaps it is because you doubt
mine. Suspicion breeds suspicion.

MAX

I'm not suspicious, sir. I'm worried. I've told you—it's the books—I just *can't* make them balance.

CONSUL

You are not supposed to keep books. (*Furious*) Books are dangerous!

MAX

I keep the figures in my head. That's why Berlin sent me. We received over a million dollars from Berlin this year. We just haven't *spent* a million.

CONSUL

And what do you think we've done with it?

MAX

I hope I've made a mistake. But I make a shortage of two hundred and fifty thousand. Those funds belonged to our country. You must help me straighten things out.

CONSUL

How can I straighten out books you keep in your head?

MAX

You will have to try, sir. (*Firmly*) I can't delay sending my report to Berlin any longer—

CONSUL

(*Turning his back on* MAX, *and in a placating voice*)
I'll do what I can, Max—

33

MAX

When?

CONSUL

Tomorrow.

MAX

No, tonight, sir. The dispatch goes back at midnight—

CONSUL

Very well, Max. (*A pause, as* MAX *gathers up all the dispatch papers.*) Max—is there nothing from London yet?

MAX

London? (*Takes an unopened letter from the pile on the table*) Why, yes—but it just looks like Schroeder—

CONSUL
(*Hastening to him*)
Give it to me! (MAX *puts a paper knife into the seal. The* CONSUL *snatches the letter*) I said, give it to me! (*Showing inscription*) "Strictly *Personal.*"

MAX

I beg your pardon. But if it's in code—

CONSUL

It won't be. Schroeder has a strange notion that codes were invented by spies to give spies employment.

MAX

A shrewd fellow.

34

CONSUL

Oh, nothing so shrewd as a loyal Nazi, educated at Oxford!
Like you, eh, Max!

MAX

Thanks. Has Schroeder been investigating somebody for
you again?

CONSUL

Ja. And what a time he took with this one! (*He deliberately
settles himself on the settee before the fireplace, fondling the
envelope, as one might play with a long-awaited love letter
before opening it.*)

MAX

(*Pointing at the letter with the paper-knife*)
Lately, sir, anybody you don't like—you suspect of being
Jewish. Forgive me, but it's become rather an obsession.

CONSUL

This can be a useful obsession for a smart Nazi. It often
solves many *personal* as well as political problems— (*Still
weighing the letter in one eager hand, he reaches over, puts
on one of his new records and turns on the phonograph. This
is a recognized gesture of dismissal to* MAX. MAX *accepts it
by picking up the dispatch-box and papers and moving to his
office door. The* CONSUL *opens the letter. At the door,* MAX
*turns.*)

MAX

The Fuehrer is broadcasting at five. Aside from Dr. Jennings, I've canceled all your appointments. You had appointments with—Jacob Berger, Hettie Rosenstein, Julia Goff and
three gentlemen called King, Kahn and Cohen.

35

CONSUL

Make them for the morning.


MAX

Let me refer them to the Embassy! Let the Embassy tell them there's no hope—

CONSUL

I'll see them in the morning. (*He has read the letter. He smiles, like an executioner who has stumbled on a bargain in axes.*)

MAX

(*Going to him suddenly*)

Sir, you do take money from these people, don't you?


CONSUL

My private income is none of your affair, Max.


MAX

I'm sorry, it is! Now, look here, sir. I'm tired of dropping gentle hints. We've got to straighten out both the finances and ethics of this Consulate. (*Raising his voice above the music which now seems to absorb the* CONSUL'S *happy attention*) Sir, you hear me?

CONSUL

Perfectly. Now, how shall I convey to you tactfully that I wish to be alone—with my letter.

> (MAX *goes to the office door again. He is about to exit, when the* CONSUL'S *short chuckle, as he reads his letter again, roots him to the spot, as if by some strange, unpleasant premonition. The* CONSUL, *sub-*

*consciously aware that the door hasn't closed, turns
and catches* MAX *staring at him fixedly.*)

MAX
(*Embarrassed*)
I—I was just listening to the music—


CONSUL
Yes, very soothing. Hitler and I also have Wagner in common.

MAX
(*Disgusted*)
That's not Wagner. That's Mendelssohn. Played by Heifetz.


CONSUL
(*Flabbergasted*)
Is it? (*Takes off record, verifies* MAX's *statement, then
smiles unexpectedly*) A *wonderful* ear you have for music!


MAX
I have, yes.

CONSUL
And your wonderful head for figures. And your persistence.
And your charming sensitivity. And your great *curiosity*. (*He
puts on another record. This time it is Wagner*—Liebestod.)


MAX
(*Abruptly*)
Sir, does that letter concern me?


CONSUL
Why should this letter concern *you*?

37

MAX

(*Realizing that if he stays for one more second he will precipitate an unpleasant scene of some sort*)
Well, I'm damned if I *know!* (*Exits to his office.*)

(*As the door closes behind* MAX, *the* CONSUL *goes to his desk. He is about to put the letter in a drawer, when something he sees through the alcove window catches his attention. He returns the letter to his pocket, picks up a pair of binoculars from the desk, and disappears for a fraction of a second behind the alcove drapes with his glasses. The door, right, opens and* SOPHIE *cautiously enters. Thinking that the room is momentarily empty, she tiptoes swiftly to the hall door, has indeed her hand on the knob, when the* CONSUL'S *voice, lilting with pleasure at having caught her out, stops her dead in her tracks.*)

CONSUL

(*Emerging from behind the curtains*)
Hello, Sophie.

SOPHIE

Oh, Karl! I didn't see you.

CONSUL

Perhaps you didn't want to.

SOPHIE

(*Her hand still on the door knob*)
Perhaps . . .

38

**CONSUL**
*(Pointing to the phonograph)*
*Liebestod.* Poor lovers. This part always breaks my heart. . . . (SOPHIE *opens the door*) Turn it off! (*She hesitates a second, then stops the machine*) You look so pretty— (*Going to her*) Where are you going?

**SOPHIE**
I—I'm just going shopping.

**CONSUL**
Please—for another parrot. But one with a less limited vocabulary. I got quite bored hearing Mr. Churchill say nothing but "Ridiculous, ridiculous, ridiculous," while I was talking at breakfast.

**SOPHIE**
Karl, you knew those grapes were poisoned.

**CONSUL**
Please, Sophie, my nerves are also tight—

**SOPHIE**
I'll be back before dinner— (*He nods pleasantly. This is an omen which quite properly makes her uneasy*) But—if you have anything special to say, Karl—

**CONSUL**
Yes. But perhaps I can say it with more assurance by dinner.

**SOPHIE**
*(Taut)*
Say it now.

39

CONSUL

I am not ready. (*He returns to the alcove, raising his binoculars.*)

SOPHIE

Oh, for God's sake, Karl, can't you ever be direct? (*Nervously*) What are you doing with those glasses?

CONSUL

Come here, Sophie.

SOPHIE

I'm not interested.

CONSUL

You will be. Come here! (*She goes to the alcove window. He hands her the glasses. Reluctantly, she looks into the street*) You see what?

SOPHIE

Nothing. The street. The police as usual.

CONSUL

Ja. There's another new policeman.

SOPHIE

Why, yes, the young one.

CONSUL

Sophie, look there— (*Turns her roughly by the shoulders*) That big man in the doorway. You recognize him?

SOPHIE

(*Putting down the binoculars defiantly*)
Yes. It's Tom Denny.

CONSUL

(*Mimicking*)

Yes, it's Tom Denny. Now why does he wait in our doorway, darling?

SOPHIE

(*Walking away from him*)

Why don't you ask him?

CONSUL

I gave Mr. Denny my full co-operation. And how does he
repay me? He spies on me. He publishes dirty articles about
me and my work. Also a few facts, which are true. And I
did not give them to him. Who did, Sophie?

SOPHIE

(*Lighting a cigarette*)

How should I know?

CONSUL

Perhaps the servants? But they do not speak one word of
English. Well, go along, Sophie. (*He rings a sharp little bell
on his desk.*)

SOPHIE

(*Flinging her hat on the settee*)

I'm not going out. I have a headache.

CONSUL

So sudden?

SOPHIE

Yes, so sudden.

CONSUL

Take an aspirin.

SOPHIE

I've just taken an aspirin.
(*Enter* MAX *from office*)

MAX

You rang, sir?

SOPHIE

And, Karl, you know what I found in your medicine chest?
(*She takes a small bottle from her purse, sniffs it*) The smell
of bitter almonds!

MAX

*What?*
(*The* CONSUL *goes quickly to her outstretched hand.
She draws back the bottle. He snatches it from her.*)

CONSUL

Thank you. (*Martyred*) You tell her, Max. (*He drops the
bottle in the downstage drawer of his desk.*)

MAX

That came in the mail yesterday. He said I mustn't tell you.
You'd be too upset—

CONSUL

(*Cheerfully*)
Probably sent by the same assassin who sent the grapes.

SOPHIE

Yesterday you got a certain poison in the mail, and this
morning my parrot dies of it. Quite a coincidence!

42

CONSUL

Life and death are often made up of such curious coincidences. Max, there is a new policeman on the hall door.

MAX

Yes, Officer Finkelstein.

CONSUL

I'm getting tired of this mayor's nasty joke. Aping La-Guardia.

MAX

Well, I am sure they're getting tired of it too, sir.

CONSUL

Max, I have noticed how very sympathetic you grow to the chosen people—in this new Zion.

MAX
(*Edgey*)

If I don't damn them every minute, you say I "sympathize." If I do, you say I protest too much.

CONSUL

Maybe I'm just jealous. After all, *you've* killed your Jew.

MAX
(*In a very flat voice*)

Yes. I've killed my Jew.

SOPHIE

Oh, Max, don't say it! Don't!

43

CONSUL

Why not? It's true, isn't it?


SOPHIE

Every time you say it, don't you see—you kill him all over again!

CONSUL

Still you never told me exactly *how* you killed him.


MAX

I don't like to talk about it.


CONSUL

Because the memory *pains* you?


MAX

No.

CONSUL

Come on, tell me. Then I'll drop the subject forever.


MAX

I'd rather drop it now.

CONSUL

Just tell me one thing. Is it true you pulled out his whiskers one by one—

MAX

(*Fiercely*)

What a monstrous lie! No! It was the night Grynszpan shot our secretary in Paris. I was in Berlin. Some of the fellows said, let's teach him—so we went down Unter den Linden. We saw an old Jew trying to board up his shop— They—

44

we all roughed him— He tried to—to hold on to me— I knocked him on the head. He fell into the gutter— He was dead when they picked him up—

CONSUL

Is that all?

MAX

Yes.

CONSUL

Now perhaps you didn't really kill him. Perhaps, if he was so very old—

MAX

No, I asked at the hospital.

CONSUL

You asked after a Jew?

MAX

Yes!

CONSUL
(*Playfully*)

Because you were sorry?

MAX

No. When they said he was dead, I was delighted!

CONSUL

As Mr. Denny would say: This boy's tough. Wouldn't he, Sophie?

SOPHIE

Oh, Max. In your heart you weren't delighted.

45

MAX

Yes, I was.

SOPHIE

You should see your face. How you *hate* yourself when you say it.

MAX

Well, damn it, nobody's glad to live in a world where he's got to kill other human beings—! (*The* CONSUL *chuckles*) That's right, laugh! So help me God, I haven't gotten around to poisoning a parrot!

CONSUL
(*Coldly*)

You think you have something on me, Max? It's always wise to have a little something on your colleague— Now, I want to interview my new Jewish Janissary!
(MAX *flings his cigarette into the fireplace, and goes into the hall, slamming the door after him.*)

SOPHIE

That was deliberately cruel. Max is the only friend you've got.

CONSUL

I am beginning to doubt his—friendship for Germany—

SOPHIE
(*Facing him*)

Now, Karl, Max is a loyal German. Though I don't believe in his heart he's a real Nazi.

CONSUL

Neither do I, Sophie.

46

SOPHIE

Some day Max will come to his senses. He'll see what you
and your kind have done to Germany.

CONSUL

I didn't realize how much you loved Germany.

SOPHIE

I want a good world. There won't be a good world until
Germany finds herself.

CONSUL

Sophie, your American mother must have been related to
Woodrow Wilson.

(*Enter* MAX, *followed by* MOE. MOE *is breezy, but
braced.*)

MAX

Officer Finkelstein.

CONSUL

(*With a contemptuous snort*)

Finkelstein.

MOE

That's me, brother.

CONSUL

We will begin by your *not* calling me brother.

MOE

Just an American way of talking. Jeez, you ain't no brother
of mine, mister!

CONSUL

Thank you.

47

MOE

Thank your mother. What a break! For both of us.


CONSUL

Shut up. (SOPHIE, *knowing what this will be like, quickly goes to the alcove, and stands there, her back to them, looking out the window*) I want to talk to you—I said I wanted to talk to you.

MOE

(*Coming well into the room with the aid of a shrug*) Well, what can I lose? This is an experience.


CONSUL

You call me "Sir."

MOE

It ain't in the book. But then, I ain't no stickler. O.K., sir.


CONSUL

Take off your hat!

MOE

That ain't in the book either— (*Takes it off.*)


MAX

Officer, this attitude won't get us anywhere.


MOE

So where do we want to get?


CONSUL

Do you know why you're here?

48

MOE

Yeah. Hizzoner the Mayor wants you to be happy—

CONSUL

What?

MOE

Hizzoner's a great guy. A great kidder. But in this instance, sir, his sense of humor stinks. Guess you agree with me.

CONSUL

It is with some reluctance I find myself agreeing with a Jew in anything—

MOE

Well, us Jews has got so many different points of view it ain't always avoidable—

CONSUL

Let us talk about the situation between you and me!

MOE

Hizzoner says I gotta watch out that no situation arises.

CONSUL

Precisely. I take it you don't like being my personal body-guard.

MOE

Well, my mother doesn't like it. But Momma's sentimental. I say, it's got its merits. Imagine me being responsible for your health. (*Grinning happily*) Now where could a cockeyed thing like this happen, except in a Democracy?

49

CONSUL

Absolutely nowhere.

MOE

Yeah. Ain't it *swell?* I mean—this is the kind of a country where you gotta defend the other guy's life and liberty with your own life, even though you *know* he ain't feeling so sweet toward your person.

CONSUL

Democracy is a good word for that. Stupidity is better.

MOE

Well, so long as I was a minority—which is what *you* are in *my* country, sir—I'd be for it.

CONSUL

Oh, I am for it—until I and what I stand for become the majority.

MOE

That I should only live so long as that will take you!

MAX

Please try to treat the Consul with respect.

MOE

We got free speech in this country. That's quite a handicap—in this instance.

CONSUL

I am annoyed that you put your solicitude for my welfare

on such altruistic grounds. This is a matter of life and death
for you.

MOE

(*Puzzled*)

How do you dope that one?

CONSUL

Do you realize what will happen to you if anything happens to me?

MOE

Sure, I get sacked off the force, if a hair of your head gets
touched— (*Twinkling as he surveys the bullet, baby-bald
head of the* CONSUL) So I got to be extra careful.

CONSUL

Shut up!

MOE

Just holding up my end of the conversation.

CONSUL

You are a Jew!

MAX

Sir, this man is an American national!

CONSUL

(*To* MAX)

Schweigen Sie! (*To* MOE) I wish to remind you of something your breed of American nationals is apt to forget. If
anything happens to me, International Jewry will be held
responsible. Have you any relatives in Germany?

51

MOE

Nope. I come of a smart family. They left long before Hitler.

CONSUL

Then all your other co-religionists everywhere in Germany will be the hostages for my safety. You remember what happened to them when Grynszpan shot our Secretary in Paris? Max, you tell him the colorful details—

MAX

You tell him. You enjoy it. (*Exits into his office, slamming that door, too.*)

MOE

(*Controlling himself*)

I know the colorful details. In this country Dillinger and Capone used to pull stunts like that. You know where they wound up. I'm hoping for the best in your case. Can I go now?

CONSUL

No. We both agree you are responsible for my safety.

MOE

Yes, sir.

CONSUL

Still you let suspicious characters hang around my house.

MOE

Kindly blueprint that.

CONSUL

(*Going toward alcove*)

There is a man in a slouch hat—out there.

52

# MARGIN FOR ERROR

MOE

Oh, the big guy? I asked Officer Solomon about him. Sol
says he's a friend of yours—

CONSUL

Why should a friend of mine wait on the sidewalk?

MOE

Maybe that's as close as a friend of yours wants to get.

CONSUL
(*Furious*)

Officer Fogelstein!

MOE

Finkelstein—Moe Finkelstein.

CONSUL

Moe—huh—Moses!

MOE

Yeah, Moses. Great guy. The original Fuehrer. (*Wistfully,
to himself*) Wish he was around now with that Big Stick
and a Red Sea handy—

CONSUL

Shut up! Tell this man I want to see him. His name is
Thomas Denny.

MOE

No kidding! Gee, next to Winchell he's getting to be my
favorite reading. Say! He's no friend of *yours*, sir!

53

CONSUL

Tell him Mr. and Mrs. Baumer want to see him.


SOPHIE

(*Distressed*)

No, Officer, tell him to go away.


CONSUL

You take orders from me.


MOE

Sorry, lady, my instructions are, I gotta do what he says.


CONSUL

Ja, you "gotta do what I says"!


MOE

Sir, your English ain't out of Shakespeare either.


CONSUL

In one minute I'll slap your face.


MOE

Listen, I've got on a uniform—


CONSUL

You should be ashamed to wear it.


MOE

(*Angry and unable to control himself any longer*)

I ain't! I wanted to wear this uniform. Ain't nobody
stuffed me into it against my will—

54

CONSUL

(*Thrusting his face into* MOE's)

I'll report you for insolence—

MOE

(*With heroic restraint, as he realizes his situation is deli-cate and his official responsibility grave*)

Listen, sir, I don't want to start nothing. A *personal* grudge against you, I ain't got. (*Letting himself go a little*) You done me a favor. You've made me see the difference between being in the land of the free and a land run by a screwball gangster. (*He turns to the door.*)

CONSUL

Hitler is a genius!

MOE

Yeah, but he's a *stupid* genius! (*The* CONSUL *moves angrily toward him.* MOE *retreats to the door*) O.K. Hitler's united Germany! But he's united everybody else's country, too. And against him.

CONSUL

(*Charging on him, raging*)

You parasite! You lousy, illiterate, poverty-stricken spawn of the Ghetto—

MOE

Sa-a-y! You got me wrong. I'm really a smart intellectual and an international banker! (*Exits quickly.*)

CONSUL

(*Foaming*)

Ach, der Tag! When it comes I'll provide His Honor the

55

Mayor with a large number of such bodyguards—to accompany him on a very long journey! (*He goes to the bar, where he moodily polishes off a glass of brandy in contemplation of this too distant millennium.*)

SOPHIE

Why did you send for Tom Denny?

CONSUL

It's more dignified to keep your rendezvous at home than on a street corner.

SOPHIE

I love Tom Denny.

CONSUL

Even a diplomat could have guessed that.

SOPHIE

Karl, please— Won't you give me a divorce?

CONSUL

Why did you marry me?

SOPHIE

(*Dully*)

Because I wanted to come back to my mother's country—and my father didn't have enough money to send me.

CONSUL

Exactly.

SOPHIE

Well, you married me because you thought the daughter of a Czech official could be useful to you—

56

CONSUL

And for the first time in my life I was a Dummkopf. (*Slaps his forehead in self-disgust*) I marry a Czech one year before Anschluss! The way things are moving in Europe, it's no longer safe to marry for anything but love—

SOPHIE

Since we're no longer of the slightest use to one another, won't you please let me go—

CONSUL

Now I see a way you may still be useful.

SOPHIE

How?

CONSUL

You have so much influence in newspaper circles—
      (MAX, *all of whose exits are precipitous, now enters
      precipitously. He is very excited, and thrusts a paper
      into the* CONSUL's *hand without ceremony.*)

MAX

Herr Consul, here is the decode. It's terribly brief— It's *very* bad news, Sophie.

SOPHIE

News from Berlin is always bad news for somebody.

CONSUL

(*Reading with* MAX's *infectious anxiety*)
Sophie! Berlin threatens to recall me—

57

SOPHIE

So they're catching up with you—


CONSUL

They give me twenty-four hours—twenty-four hours—
(*Crumples paper and tosses it on the desk*) to get rid of
Horst, establish more favorable relations with the press . . .


MAX

And clear up the finances of this office!
(SOPHIE *laughs.*)

SOPHIE

What, no order to overthrow the government at Washington?

MAX

Sophie, this is serious for all of us—


CONSUL

Max, I will explain to her how serious it is. (MAX *exits. The*
CONSUL *waits until the door closes, quickly, and then says in
an ominous voice*) You know what'll happen to me if I go
back? (*He's frightened himself*) The Third Reich allows no
margin for error!

SOPHIE

I ought to say I'm sorry, but I'm not.


CONSUL

Perhaps I will not have to go. I can manage Horst. I foresaw that. But our finances . . . Sophie, our books don't balance. There is quite a shortage—

58

SOPHIE

Well, Karl, what have you done with the money?

CONSUL

I? Max is handling all the money.

SOPHIE
(*Laughing derisively*)

Oh, stop it! You are. Max can prove that to Berlin.

CONSUL

Who's going to take his word against mine in Berlin—
*now?*

SOPHIE

Now?

CONSUL

Imagine, our charming Max's English grandmother was a
full-blooded Jewess!

SOPHIE
(*Aghast*)

It's not true!

CONSUL
(*Stroking his breast pocket gratefully*)

I've a letter from my London agent. Carefully documented.

SOPHIE

But, Karl, they'd send him to a camp—

CONSUL
(*Mournfully*)

That's routine, Sophie.

SOPHIE

You can't tell him! He couldn't stand it. He might—
(*Horrified*) *do* something to himself.


CONSUL

Ja. Tch. Sensitive fellow. Only way out, and all that?
Still, that would dispose of the shortage—and Max.


SOPHIE

Oh, you can't get away with that! (*Fiercely*) I won't let
you—I'm going to warn Max—


CONSUL

Sophie, don't meddle. You're going to need all your clever
little mind to take care of yourself— And now, your romantic
Mr. Denny. You will inform him that his articles have made
it necessary for *you* to go home with me—


SOPHIE

But I won't go!

CONSUL

Then Berlin will have you deported.


SOPHIE

No!

CONSUL

Ja! Listen, Sophie—you'll tell Mr. Denny this. (*He circles
about the room, like a man composing a short but clever
death warrant*) And he'll say—"Is there nothing you can
do?" And you'll say—"Nothing. My husband's been a failure."

60

And you'll say—"But, but, if he just had a good press—for some time—until this tragic affair of Max is forgotten—"

SOPHIE

You're improvising. You *are* desperate!

CONSUL

(*Truthful for once*)

Do you think *I* want to go back to Germany any more than you do? It is an easier country to serve than live in—just between us.

SOPHIE

You mean you'll send me back unless I help you ruin Max!

CONSUL

(*Persuasively.*)

But Max is no longer one of us.

SOPHIE

I'd rather *die* than do that!

CONSUL

If you don't let me handle this, you *will* die.

SOPHIE

Perhaps you'll kill me—

CONSUL

I, Sophie? (*The surprise of this unkind accusation causes him to drop his monocle as if it were a hypocritical tear*) You are an informer. *Berlin* knows what to do with traitors.

61

SOPHIE

I don't care what happens to me!

CONSUL

Don't forget—your father's in Prague. I've protected him.
He's not exactly free, but he's *alive*.

SOPHIE

(*Hysterically*)

I deserve to die, just for having lived with a swine like
you!

CONSUL

(*Cheerful again*)

So don't try any tricks. Don't run away with your romantic
reporter. It might save you, but it won't save Max and it certainly won't be so nice for your dear papa.

(SOPHIE *flings herself sobbing on the settee as* MAX
*enters at the hall door.*)

MAX

Dr. Jennings is here—

SOPHIE

(*Rising and rushing to him*)

Max, listen. Be careful.

CONSUL

(*Warningly*)

Sophie!

SOPHIE

We must both be terribly careful!

62

CONSUL

Sophie—*don't meddle!*

SOPHIE

He's got to have a scapegoat, but we can beat him! Don't believe anything he says.

CONSUL

You'll order passage for Sophie on the *Bremen.*

SOPHIE

(*Throwing herself into* MAX's *bewildered arms*)
No! I won't go! I won't go back to Germany! (*The* CONSUL *goes to her, grabs her wrist, to pull her away.*)

MAX

(*As she clings to him*)
Damn it, Baumer, I won't have this!

CONSUL

(*Pushing him roughly aside*)
From now on, things will be the way *I* want!

SOPHIE

(*Beside herself with physical terror*)
Let me go! (*He gives her arm a painful jerk, she pulls it free, and, flinging open the door, rushes into the hall, where* DR. JENNINGS, *hearing this unpleasant racket, is standing in some bewilderment*) Oh, Doctor—Doctor Jennings! Can't you help—can't somebody help!

DR. JENNINGS

Mrs. Baumer, please! (*He has his arms about her, and pro-*

63

*pels her back into the room, patting her shoulder, hugging
her a little to quiet her sobs.*)


CONSUL

Forgive her, Doctor. A domestic situation. And the worst
thing about this situation is the scene she's making of it.


DR. JENNINGS

She needs a sedative. Would you permit me?


CONSUL

She is often this way.


DR. JENNINGS

Well, that is hardly reassuring. My bag is in the reception
room, Baron.

MAX

I'll get it, Doctor. (*He exits into hall.*)


DR. JENNINGS

My dear child, go to your room. I'll be with you in a
minute. (SOPHIE, *exits. The doctor, coldly professional again,
turns to the* CONSUL, *who has successfully recovered his aplomb
during the obbligato of* SOPHIE'S *hysterical outburst*) Do you
care to tell me the cause of her hysteria?


CONSUL

Well, she's under tension. We live in a dangerous atmosphere. Our lives are threatened daily.

64

DR. JENNINGS

I can imagine.

(*Enter* FRIEDA *quickly.*)

FRIEDA

Herr Consul, ist *Frau Baumer* krank?

CONSUL

Ja. Bleiben Sie mit *Frau Baumer*— (FRIEDA *exits after* SOPHIE) Only yesterday and again this morning I received deadly poison in my mail.

DR. JENNINGS

It should be easy to trace the sender. Deadly poisons are not easy to come by.

CONSUL

Cyanide? It can be bought in any photographer's store. It is used for developing.

(*Enter* MAX *with the doctor's bag, which he hands to him.*)

DR. JENNINGS

It's rarely used for murder. Acts too quickly. It's the suicide's poison.

CONSUL

The suicide's poison? That's interesting, isn't it, Max?

MAX

(*Avoiding the* CONSUL's *compelling gaze*)

Yes, very.

65

DR. JENNINGS

Baumer, I came here about Professor Norberg. I want your final answer when I come back.

CONSUL

You shall have it.

DR. JENNINGS

Thank you. (*Exits. There is a brief pause. Then* MAX *quietly and closely faces the* CONSUL.)

MAX

What did she mean that you needed a scapegoat?

CONSUL

(*Grinning*)

You tell *me*, Max.

MAX

Very well. Now what have you done with that two hundred fifty thousand?

CONSUL

(*Sadly*)

The stock market. Max, the Third Reich allows no margin for error—but Wall St. requires a very big one. I was sold out.

MAX

What damn stupidity! Why, even Americans have stopped playing the market—

CONSUL

(*Going to the bar for a bracer*)

Max, when I came to this country and saw how rich it was, I said—how much richer will it be under National Socialism.

So I played the market long. But democracies are perverse.
Every time our Fuehrer opened his mouth—down this market
tumbled! You can draw your report for Berlin now.
(*A pause.*)

MAX

But you're my friend—

CONSUL
(*Happily*)

I am a traitor.

MAX
(*Bewildered*)

There are human relationships!

CONSUL
(*With cast-iron slyness*)

Max, this smells like *appeasement!*

MAX

Appeasement?

CONSUL

Yes. One might suspect there's something you are frightened about yourself—

MAX
(*Grimly*)

Now what's in that letter?

CONSUL
(*Waggling a finger*)

Can't you guess, Max?

67

MAX

(*Terrified*)

Look here, Schroeder can't know anything about my English grandmother. I've already tried to find out myself. I—

CONSUL

Ja. One's blood begins to ask questions—

MAX

(*Hysterically*)

There's no answer in my blood that says I do not belong to Germany, that Germany does not belong to me.

CONSUL

Isn't there?

MAX

For God's sake, sir! You know I love Germany. (*He is standing now, very close to the bust of his Fuehrer*) I love all *he* has done for it. He gave us back our honor, our belief in the beauty of our own traditions—

CONSUL

(*Bored*)

Please, Max, this is *not* a Nuremberg rally—

MAX

It's not true! It can't be. (*His whole person seems to be warding off a horrible physical assault*) I couldn't bear it!

68

CONSUL
(*Sympathetically*)
Of course not. Life would be intolerable— (*Hopefully*)
Wouldn't it? (*He takes out the letter, to clinch the matter
of* MAX's *inability to bear this truth, by showing it to him.*)

MAX
Yes. . . . (*And now he sees the eager expectancy in the*
CONSUL's *eyes*) Why, damn you! That letter is a *trick*. You're
just trying to make me the scapegoat, so you won't have to
go back to Germany. (*He grabs the* CONSUL *by the throat
with a young strong hand*) Give me that letter!

CONSUL
(*Struggling*)
Lassen Sie mich!

MAX
(*Shaking him fiercely*)
Give it to me! (*During this brief struggle neither of them
has seen* HORST *enter, five fingers outthrust first in a Nazi
salute.*)

HORST
Heil Hitler! (*Amazed*) Come, boys! What goes on here?
(*They break apart. The* CONSUL *fishes for his monocle and
straightens his tie and, smoothing the letter, tucks it again
into his breast pocket.* MAX *gives* HORST *a wild-eyed stare, and
goes quickly into his office,* HORST *trotting angrily after him*)
Baron von Alvenstor! He is your superior. You will explain—

CONSUL

He will explain to me, Horst.

HORST

(*Coming back*)

What's this all about?

CONSUL

Nothing. A little bad news from London about his grandmother. He's overwrought. I am really afraid he will harm himself.

HORST

It looked more like he was going to harm you.

CONSUL

My life is very safe if all I have to fear is this neurotic. (*Quite composed again, and looking for new fields to plow under*) Well, how did the rally go?

HORST

Short but thrilling.

CONSUL

A big crowd?

HORST

One hundred and sixty-three in the hall. And about one thousand in the streets.

CONSUL

Trying to get in?

HORST

No. Waiting for me to come out.

CONSUL

And the photographers?

HORST

They lay down on their stomachs to take shots of me—
You know, the angle that does libelous things to my nostrils.

CONSUL

And the people you hired to throw things at you?

HORST

(*Indignant*)

They didn't throw them, the Judases!—Then the police
simply melted them. I tell you, in America the protection of
discontented minorities amounts to a political monopoly—

(*Enter* MOE, *followed at a wary amble by* THOMAS
DENNY. DENNY *is a successful newspaper columnist in
his early thirties. His affected carelessness of attire
merely underscores his self-assured masculine appeal.
He is tall, tousle-haired, and highly irreverent in the
presence of any form of official presumption. His
loathing for* MR. BAUMER *is outweighed only by his
love for* SOPHIE. *For his delicate role in the lives of
these people he has assumed a tone of equivocal
banter, which collapses only during certain bitter
moments, when he recognizes that his own good in-
tentions are an insufficient shield for the protection
of* SOPHIE.)

MOE

Mr. Baumer, here's your suspicious-looking character.
(*Exits.*)

71

DENNY

Hello, Baumer. (*To* HORST) Oh, good morning, dear teacher. How did your ring-around-the-rally go? Aw— Nobody chuck a big red apple at you?

HORST

(*Loftily*)

I won't demean myself to reply to your snotty remarks. But make a note of this—I have *you* on my index!

DENNY

At last, I'm in the Who's Who of America.

CONSUL

(*Suavely*)

Mr. Denny, will you excuse us? We have a little important business.

DENNY

O.K. I'll make it mine, later. (*Exits.*)

HORST

Important? (*Eagerly*) Are there any orders for me from Berlin?

CONSUL

Yes, Horst.

HORST

And some money?

CONSUL

You are not going to need money.

72

HORST

Now, look here. My expenses are heavy. These uniforms—
(*Takes a wicked-looking knife from the sheath at his belt*)
And I've ordered four thousand of these knives. They're in-
scribed, too—"Blut und Ehre"—"Blood and Honor." (*The*
CONSUL *takes the knife, examining it thoughtfully*) The
handle is of cork—leaves no finger-prints—

CONSUL

We will have the words changed to "Country and Honor."
(*Drops the knife on the low table beside the sofa.*)

HORST

Why?

CONSUL

Orders from Berlin.

HORST

I don't agree with this new policy of playing down Ger-
manic words. Our primary objective is to spread Germanic
Kultur— (*Whips gun from his hip pocket triumphantly*)
That's why from now on I carry a gun!

CONSUL
(*Coldly*)

Have you a permit?

HORST

You know they won't let us have anything in the camps
but BB rifles!

CONSUL

Give that to me.

73

HORST

No. I want it.

CONSUL

(*Snatching it, and breeching it*)

Loaded.

HORST

(*Surprised*)

No—is it?

CONSUL

Dummkopf! (*Puts gun beside knife*) Once you were almost sent up for drunken driving.

HORST

I asked for good pale Hofbrau. (*Injured*) But those Tennessee Legionnaires played me a dirty trick—they gave me something called Hell Hole Swamp Water!

CONSUL

And once you nearly got yourself sent up for perjury.

HORST

But isn't it also my manifest destiny to go to jail (*Pointing to Hitler's bust*) like *he* did?

CONSUL

Horst, you're finished.

HORST

How dare you say that to me?

CONSUL

At first, you made a convincing noise. But now you are

74

obscuring our great Nazi truths— You have become a national comic-strip!

HORST
(*Furious*)
When I come to power, Karl Baumer, I shall *purge* you!


CONSUL
Now, don't take this personally. I, too, take orders—from Berlin.

HORST
But the press, the people, just laugh at me! That's a terribly discouraging atmosphere for social revolution! Let me carry my gun— (*Reaches for it, and the* CONSUL *slaps his fat hand away*) Well, what *can* I do?


CONSUL
(*Pleasantly*)
Find a martyr.

HORST
A martyr?

CONSUL
(*Patiently*)
A martyr's one who will *die* for his beliefs.


HORST
Oh, I've often just stuck my head right into a crowd, positively inviting disaster.

CONSUL
My dear Horst, if you could contrive to get yourself—how do they say it here—rubbed out by a—Jew!

75

HORST

Oh, don't be ridiculous! How do I contrive to get myself—rubbed out by a Jew? (*Sauntering, with jolly complacency, away from the* CONSUL) Their self-restraint is positively nauseating! Ha! Ha!

CONSUL

Now, perhaps I could arrange it for you.
(HORST's *laugh suddenly freezes. He spins around and faces the* CONSUL.)

HORST
(*Whispering*)
What did you say, Baumer?

CONSUL

I said *I* could arrange it.

HORST
(*Stunned*)
But—I—who—if the American Fuehrer dies—

CONSUL
(*Reassuringly*)
We will replace you.

HORST
(*His uncritical belief in his heroic destiny is suffering a terrible strain*)
You're trying to murder me! I won't have it! If Berlin's so hard up for a martyr, let them send one over! And they'd better send someone to kill him—

CONSUL

Is the American Fuehrer not prepared to die for his Nazi principles?

HORST

(*Incoherent with fear*)

No!!! I mean—yes—I—I mean, I haven't finished my memoirs yet, I—

CONSUL

The Fuehrer asks nobody to do what he wouldn't do himself.

HORST

Yes, but so far nobody has asked him— (*Coming very close to the* CONSUL) Look here, what about *you?*

CONSUL

(*Genuinely surprised*)

Me?

HORST

Yes. You! This house is surrounded by Jews! You always have them available!

CONSUL

(*Thoughtfully*)

Yes. I have a Moe Finkelstein.

HORST

(*Eagerly*)

Yes! And *you* are much more important than *I* am!

CONSUL

Horst, this is no time for modesty.

77

HORST

Now don't try to pull any of your Berlin high-jinks on me! You're a real German. My parents were just born over there—accidentally. Milwaukee is my home! Milwaukee just isn't Munich. Why—why— (*This is a beautiful and opportune discovery*) I'm an *American!*

CONSUL

My dear Horst! I didn't mean to frighten you. (*Waves him to the easy chair, as he goes to the bar for another brandy*) Relax a moment. Get used to the idea. And I will arrange all the troublesome details for you.

HORST
(*Craftily*)

Have you a scheme?

CONSUL

Not worked out yet. But your cork-handled knife, for instance, which leaves no fingerprints.

HORST

What about it?

CONSUL

If you were found with it, in your back in my hallway late tonight—

HORST
(*Terrified*)

Have you already hired someone to assassinate me?

CONSUL

Whom could I trust but *myself*, Horst?

## MARGIN FOR ERROR

HORST

(*Waggling a trembling finger*)

Isn't this very risky?

CONSUL

(*Laughing*)

For you or for me, Horst? (*Persuasively*) When you were discovered I should simply say you had a quarrel this afternoon with my Jewish policeman—

HORST

But I haven't—

CONSUL

Just hang around. I will arrange one.

HORST

(*Desperate*)

But—suppose you couldn't *prove* the policeman did it?

CONSUL

All that is necessary is that *he* should not be able to prove he *didn't*.

HORST

Look here, suppose they suspect you?

CONSUL

(*This interview is now over, as far as the* CONSUL *is concerned. He goes to the hall door.*)

Why should anyone suspect me of murdering you any more than they would suspect you of murdering me?

79

HORST

*(Thoughtfully, to* BAUMER's *back)*
There's something *in* that thought, Baumer—


CONSUL

*(Calling into hall)*
Mr. Denny, I am ready for *you* now. Horst *(Waving him toward the office)*, the Fuehrer broadcasts in ten minutes. That always gives me further inspiration. Afterward, we will discuss my inspiration—

HORST

*(Cunningly)*
And mine too. *(Salutes with vigorous confidence)* Heil Hitler! *(Exits into office as* DENNY *enters.)*


DENNY

So you have no dealings with that tin-horn Hitler?


CONSUL

You hold a low opinion of our American leader.


DENNY

Every cause gets the leader it deserves.


CONSUL

I take that as a great compliment to our cause in Germany.


DENNY

But some causes can't stand transplanting.

CONSUL

We don't transplant. We sow good seeds which propagate naturally.

DENNY

Baumer, we can't argue. We begin from opposite premises. You believe the citizen was born to serve the state. We believe the citizen is the state—

CONSUL

Our belief has created a great Germany.

DENNY

All the returns on Germany are not in yet. Don't forget. America's still the richest and freest nation.

CONSUL

I hope you can defend this fat Eden.

DENNY

Any time you don't think so, just try to come and get it!

CONSUL

Then it may be too late. By that time America may have caught the disease which has weakened its sister democracies. The little disease they picked up in Munich—

DENNY

Oh, we're thinking about that too, Baumer.

CONSUL

Fortunately, that's all you Americans do, is think!

81

DENNY

Well, we've had the habit for a couple of centuries. We've got the biggest Brain Trust in the world, one hundred and thirty million people who can all do their *own* thinking.

CONSUL

Such a wasted effort, when your President Rosenfeld is determined to do it for them.

DENNY

O.K. But who checks even the President's thinking? (*Kidding his way out of a tense, trite and fruitless discussion*) The most fearless and uncensored journalists, who, I am proud to say, all violently and publicly disagree with one another. But there's one thing we don't disagree about— (*Seriously*) we just don't like *you*. Now, the officer said Mrs. Baumer also wanted to see me.

CONSUL

Yes. But she's not well now. She's had a slight shock. Or, should I say I have had a slight shock? Berlin is about to recall me.

(DENNY's *mouth relaxes in a happy grin.*)

DENNY

That's dandy.

CONSUL

Thanks to your articles.

DENNY

May I quote you?

82

CONSUL

Still, there's an "out" for me which might be acceptable to
Berlin.

DENNY

(*Cheerfully*)

Right now I'm having no part of it.

CONSUL

You're afraid you would lose your job if you changed your
views?

DENNY

(*Laughing*)

Oh, yes. That has me terrified.

CONSUL

Let me be very frank. Headline news may burst out of this
office before midnight. I'd like you to cover it—with sympathy. Mr. Denny, there's $50,000 in that safe. Let me con-
clude this talk by giving it to you.

DENNY

You know how I'm going to head off my Sunday column?
"Berlin offers its entire gold reserve for a few kind words
from your correspondent."

CONSUL

(*Icily*)

I'm afraid you don't quite understand this situation, Mr.
Denny. It seems my wife is in love with you—
      (*A pause.* DENNY *is visibly unprepared for the* CONSUL's
      *knowledge.*)

DENNY

Well, that's excellent news. (*Stalling*) I knew she liked me, but—

CONSUL

(*Evenly*)

Have a drink, Denny?

DENNY

(*Uneasily*)

Thanks. A Scotch, straight, is indicated—

CONSUL

(*Pouring drinks*)

I take brandy the same way—a taste acquired in the tropics. I was Consul in British South Africa. Now, this question of the colonies—

DENNY

(*Directly*)

Sophie tell you she loved me?

CONSUL

No. I told her. (*Hands him drink with a courtly gesture.*)

DENNY

Listen, Baumer, Sophie and I have never— Well, we love one another, yes—but—

CONSUL

I'm a gentleman. I don't ask embarrassing questions.

DENNY

There are times when you're *not* a gentleman if you don't ask them!

CONSUL

My wife sails on the *Bremen*.

DENNY

I'll give odds she doesn't.

CONSUL

Then I'll have her deported.

DENNY

We'll see about that—

CONSUL

Mr. Denny, Berlin is recalling me because certain facts have leaked out of my office. Now, in self-defense I will have to explain that my wife was your informer. And Berlin has such a brutal custom. They use *axes* on little ladies' necks in Berlin— (DENNY *looks into the* CONSUL's *cold, determined face just long enough to see that he means that. He tosses off his drink and slowly puts the glass on the bar.*)

DENNY

Well, Baumer, you've found my price. (*Grimly*) But I've got to think it over. I have a feeling now I'd rather shoot you than deliver.

(*Enter* DR. JENNINGS.)

DR. JENNINGS

I beg your pardon—

CONSUL

(*Pleasantly*)

Dr. Jennings, Mr. Denny—

85

DR. JENNINGS
(*Shaking hands*)
How do you do? Glad to know *you*—

CONSUL
How is my wife?
(*The doctor sits in the easy chair and writes a prescription on the low table.*)

DR. JENNINGS
In medical terms, she's suffering from a compulsion neurosis— A persecution complex which demands she solve her apparently unsolvable problems quickly.

CONSUL
Ja, the same neurosis that torments most of Europe.

DR. JENNINGS
(*Seeing breached gun*)
Baumer, I wouldn't leave a loaded weapon handy. Peace conferences are best held in an atmosphere of disarmament.

CONSUL
I am not afraid of a woman.

DR. JENNINGS
I am thinking of what she might do to herself.

DENNY
(*Exploding*)
I want to see Sophie.

86

DR. JENNINGS
(*Gently*)

Not now, boy. I've given her a sedative. In a few minutes—

CONSUL

In the waiting room, Mr. Denny. I want you to see her, too. You *must* ask her about her father—

DENNY

I'd like to bust you in the nose right now.

DR. JENNINGS
(*Casually*)

I'll be leaving in just a moment. (DENNY *exits. The doctor rises and goes to the* CONSUL, *who has picked up the knife and the gun from the small table, and during the following scene drops them casually on the top of his desk*) It's useless to warn you further about your wife—

CONSUL
(*Wearily*)

We have exhausted the subject—

DR. JENNINGS

And now what about the Norbergs?

CONSUL

Your friend Professor Norberg has been released. He is now in Dusseldorf and will soon be on his way to America.

DR. JENNINGS

Thank God!

CONSUL

(*Rings bell on desk*)

My secretary will give you the affidavits— (*As the doctor moves to the office door*) One minute, Doctor, let me ask you a question— (MAX *enters*) We—you and I—are Aryans, yes?

DR. JENNINGS

That word has no meaning for the scientist.

CONSUL

That's a quibble. Let's say we are Christians.

DR. JENNINGS

We have some intimations of God. Are we Christians?

CONSUL

At least we are not *Jews!* Doctor, just between these walls, do you really like them?

DR. JENNINGS

Baumer, I'm a doctor. I can't think of human beings in such unscientific terms as Aryan or non-Aryan. I only think of them as healthy human beings or ill ones. As a medical man, I have seen that sufferers are not the most pleasant people to be with, or the easiest to deal with. Even you will not deny that the Jews have suffered, and are still suffering abominably. They are sick! Sick with the most cruel disease that can attack man's body or soul—fear of his fellows. I marvel that a people so persecuted, so humiliated, have borne themselves with so much pride and decency and fortitude and humor—

88

CONSUL

Isn't that a long-winded way to say you don't like them?

DR. JENNINGS

It's a long-winded way to say that in the eternal war of nerves against Jewry, we've been the aggressors—

CONSUL

And we will be the victors! Eh, Max?

MAX

I wonder—

CONSUL

Now, Doctor, there still remains this annoying question of Norberg's passage money.

DR. JENNINGS

I've already given you five thousand dollars.

CONSUL

It seems some officials just put that in their pockets.

DR. JENNINGS

So bribes are taken, even in the Third Reich?

CONSUL

Only by Jews, Doctor.

DR. JENNINGS
(*Sarcastic*)

Oh, there are still Jewish officials in the Third Reich?

CONSUL

Not who admit it. But Berlin realized at once, when they took bribes, that they were Jews, so Berlin purged them. A blank check, Max, for the doctor.

DR. JENNINGS

This is the damnedest blackmail. I won't give you another penny!

CONSUL
(*Shrugging*)
Then there will be a delay in the professor's leaving Hamburg—

DR. JENNINGS
(*Urgently*)
Listen, Baumer, it was very difficult for me to raise that five thousand dollars. (*A pause*) I only did it because—Norberg's my son-in-law—Mrs. Norberg is my daughter—

CONSUL

Your *daughter?*

DR. JENNINGS
Yes. My only daughter.

CONSUL
(*With a qualm, faint but fleeting*)
Why didn't you tell me this before?

DR. JENNINGS
I'm a good judge of human nature. I knew if this was a racket—the fact she was my daughter would make it more costly—

90

CONSUL

You are too hard on me. (*Magnanimously*) We will waive the question of the passage money!

DR. JENNINGS
(*Smiling*)

Thank you.

CONSUL

Max, give him the affidavits and the memo on Norberg that came this morning.

MAX
(*Appalled*)

You really want me to give him that?

CONSUL

Why not?

MAX
(*Stalling*)

It's in German. (*To the doctor*) I'll mail it to you.

DR. JENNINGS

You can translate it for me.

MAX

That would take some time—

DR. JENNINGS

I'll wait gladly!

(MAX *looks desperately from the smiling doctor to the* CONSUL's *cold dead-pan. Then, nervously, he goes to the radio, turns the dial.*)

MAX

But, Doctor, it's almost time for the broadcast—
(*The doctor sets his jaw stubbornly. The* CONSUL *shrugs at* MAX.)

CONSUL

Doctor, please wait in the reception room—

DR. JENNINGS

(*Suspicious, bewildered*)
What's the matter with you two? You're playing me some trick. I don't leave this house until I have definite proof that my son-in-law and my daughter are out of that camp.

CONSUL

In the reception room, Doctor.

DR. JENNINGS

By God, Baumer, if this *is* a trick—if any harm comes to my girl— (*Exits to hall. Through the bitter silence that now lies between* MAX *and the* CONSUL, *a voice comes.*)

RADIO ANNOUNCER

. . . At 5 o'clock, bringing you Adolf Hitler on an International hookup. Until then we bring you a program of transcribed music. Strauss' waltz, "Wine, Women and Song!"— (*And the strains of this happy waltz grotesquely break the tension.*)

CONSUL

Max, break it to him gently—

MAX

(*Furiously*)

It's the last piece of dirty work I do for you. (*Goes to office*)
Baumer, you can forget appeasement. You can't buy my loyalty to Germany. No matter what's in that letter, I send my
report at midnight. (*Exits.*)

CONSUL

Max, this patriotism will undo you. (*Enter* FRIEDA) Geht es
Frau Baumer besser?

FRIEDA

Ein bischen, Herr Consul.

> (CONSUL *exits. It is quite dark in the room now.* FRIEDA
> *goes to the switch, turns up the lights, as* MOE *enters
> from the hall. He surveys the room, grins at* FRIEDA,
> *who again studiously ignores him and goes to draw
> the alcove curtains.*)

MOE

Hey, toots! Where's the Consul?

FRIEDA

Der Consul?

MOE

Yeah.

FRIEDA

Bei Frau Baumer.

MOE

With Mrs. Baumer?

FRIEDA

Ja.

MOE

Jeez, I'm startin' to understand German. Listen, honey!
Tell the Consul there's some ugly-lookin' customers in the
street—

FRIEDA

(*Snootily*)

Ich will mit ihnen nichts zu tun haben.

MOE

Yeah. No one should leave the house. Baumer is about to
be serenaded.

FRIEDA

Was?

MOE

Serenaded! (*Goes to window. Now from the street we hear
a faint murmur of voices. People are gathering there.* MOE
*points out the window*) Boo! Hiss! (*Gives a loud Bronx
cheer*) Get it?

FRIEDA

(*The pantomime has been informative*)

Ja! Ich werde es dem Herrn Konsul sagen— (*She moves
to door.*)

MOE

Hey! Wait, baby—

FRIEDA

(*Pausing*)

Was?

MOE

(*Going to her*)

You're a darn cute-lookin' kid. How'd *you* ever get mixed
up with these bums?

94

FRIEDA

*(Uppish)*

Ich verstehe Sie nicht.

MOE

*(With a sincerity that transcends all the barriers of race and language)*

You're beautiful!

FRIEDA

*(Smiling cutely)*

Meinen Sie?

MOE

Aw, you dames understand *that* in any language! Listen, your eyes— *(Pantomiming)* Dietrich! Your shape—Hedy Lamarr! Your lips—Loretta Young—

FRIEDA

*(Pouting)*

Nein. Greta Garbo!

MOE

O.K. We'll settle for Garbo. Now, how's for heatin' me up a cup of coffee?

FRIEDA

Kaffee? Der *Officer Solomon* will auch immer Kaffee!

MOE

Baby, look out for Officer Solomon— He's married!

FRIEDA

Was?

95

MOE
*(Pointing to her ring finger)*
Married! *(Pantomiming the ascending steps of the Solomon progeny)* Five Solomons— *(Pantomiming)* more comin'.


FRIEDA
Married? *(Pointing at his ring finger)* Sie—married?


MOE
*(Hurt)*
Who, me? No, God forbid.


FRIEDA
*(Flirting and pointing to his costume)*
Eine schöne uniform!

MOE
Say, toots, how about the two of us steppin' out tonight?


FRIEDA
*(Bewildered)*
Ich verstehe Sie nicht.

MOE
Hold on a minute. *(Goes to* CONSUL's *desk)* I'll find a calendar.

FRIEDA
*(Frightened and suspicious)*
Was machen Sie denn bei dem Schreibtisch?


MOE
*(Placating as he searches the top of the desk)*
I'm looking for a *calendar.*

96

FRIEDA

Kalender?

MOE

Guess these guys don't need a calendar. Their time marches backwards— (*Nevertheless, he has found one. He brings it back to* FRIEDA *and shows her the date*) Now, then, duchess, are you free for dinner—*tonight?*

FRIEDA

Nein. Heute muss ich Fuehrer's Radio zuhören.

MOE

(*Misunderstanding*)

Jeez! You don't have to get Hitler's permission? Well, **how** about Saturday night? Seven o'clock—

FRIEDA

Sieben Uhr?—Gut!

MOE

(*Pantomimes*)

First we eat? Blintzes? Lotkes?

FRIEDA

(*Shaking her head*)

Nein. Keine Blintzes—Chop Suey!

MOE

O.K. Chop Suey.

FRIEDA

Movies?

MOE

Sure—"Confessions of a Nazi Spy"?

FRIEDA

Ja.

MOE

O.K., Toots, it's a date. (*Pats her cheek, delicately.*)

FRIEDA
(*Warily*)

Und *denn* was?

MOE

Denn was? Then it's up to you, baby.

FRIEDA
(*Pointing to the radio, which all this while has been playing its merry waltz*)

Tantzen?

MOE

Sure thing. (*Soft-shoeing*) The Fred Astaire of Spring 3100—

FRIEDA
(*Admiringly*)

Schön! Schön! (*Opening her arms*) Tantzen mit mir?

MOE

Why does anybody learn to talk? It ain't really necessary! (*He grabs her gaily in his arms and whirls her into a happy spinning waltz about the room.*)

98

FRIEDA
(*Counting as they spin*)
Eins, zwei, drei, eins, zwei, drei.


MOE
(*Blissfully*)
Jeez! Just like the good old days in Vienna.
(*Enter* CONSUL. *Obviously to him this is by far the most outrageous thing that has happened that day in his Consulate.*)

CONSUL
(*Bellowing*)
Finkelstein! What's going on here?
(MOE, *with enormous presence of mind, whirls* FRIEDA, *squeaking with fear, out of the room, into the hall, and returns to face the* CONSUL's *wrath alone.*)


MOE
(*Placating*)
Oh, just a quiet little Anschluss—
(*Enter* DENNY, *grinning, behind* MOE.)


CONSUL
Trying to seduce beautiful blonde Aryan girls!


DENNY
That's right. He—and *all* the rest of us!


MOE
(*Warmly*)
Thanks, brother. (*Exits quickly, as* SOPHIE *enters.* DENNY's

*smile fades as he sees her. The* CONSUL *looks from one to the other, and their patent unhappiness restores his complacency.*)

CONSUL
(*Cheerfully*)
Now, I will give you two one and a half minutes for a final tête-à-tête—

DENNY
(*Grimly*)
After which comes the Blitzkrieg?

CONSUL
A charming parallel. In one and a half minutes, the Fuehrer will speak to all loyal Germans everywhere, and all private matters will have to be suspended. Auf Wiedersehen— (*Exits to office.*)

SOPHIE
(*Going to* DENNY)
Darling! Darling! I'm so frightened—

DENNY
(*Taking her firmly in his arms*)
Now let's see. What's the *worst* that can happen?

SOPHIE
I'll have to go back with him, or they'll kill my father—

DENNY
O.K. Neither of those things is going to happen. I've got a little scheme.

SOPHIE

What is it?

DENNY

You'll know all about it tomorrow—

SOPHIE

(*Hysterically*)

Tomorrow I may be on the *Bremen.*

DENNY

(*Gently*)

You *won't* be—

SOPHIE

But if they kidnap me? They've done things like that.

DENNY

Now get this! Before I let him ship you off, *I'll* kill him.

SOPHIE

(*Fiercely*)

And I'd help you!

DENNY

(*Soothingly*)

Darling, the Peace Front. That's what we are—

SOPHIE

But, Tom, what about my father?

DENNY

There'll be no end to that blackmail, ever, unless you say, here's an end to it—

**SOPHIE**

But your plan—it does include him?

**DENNY**

(*Grimly*)

My plan will settle everything—

**SOPHIE**

(*Whispering*)

You *are* going to—to kill him!

**DENNY**

I would—if it were necessary. But the first step is for us to get the hell out of here. *Now.*

**SOPHIE**

(*Walking away from him, distraught*)

I can't let Max down—

**DENNY**

What the hell has Max got to do with this?

**SOPHIE**

Karl found out today that Max is partly Jewish.

**DENNY**

Sounds like a lucky break for the Baron.

**SOPHIE**

Karl has been stealing money. Now he can blame it on Max.

102

**DENNY**

He's rigged it so that Max takes the rap for him?

**SOPHIE**

Oh, it's worse. He's trying to make Max commit suicide.

**DENNY**

So that's what he means by headline news breaking out of here before midnight.

**SOPHIE**

Yes! We've got to stand by Max—*I* must be the one to tell him. Karl must let me.

**DENNY**

Your sweet husband won't give that pleasure up. He's an A-number one chop-licker.

**SOPHIE**

(*With pathetic reasonableness*)

But it's such a little thing to ask. He can't be that inhuman.

**DENNY**

Must I rise to his defense? He's an incorruptible bastard.

(*The radio waltz ends abruptly.*)

**RADIO ANNOUNCER**

We are now on the air for an international broadcast—

**DENNY**

(*Grimacing*)

Oh, boy! Now we're in for a dose of Mr. Schicklegruber!

(*Turns off radio with a gesture of distaste.*)

103

SOPHIE

Schicklegruber?

DENNY

Schicklegruber, that's Adolf's *real* name. His mother's name.
His father never gave him one, as everyone realizes intuitively.
Just think, history might have been different if he hadn't
changed it to Hitler!

SOPHIE

Why?

DENNY

(*With an enormous farcical salute*)
Heil Schicklegruber!

SOPHIE

(*Smiling for the first time*)
How silly!

DENNY

Whenever you're frightened, darling, of all that Hitler
stands for, just *think* Heil Schicklegruber!

SOPHIE

Tom—your plan isn't *just* "Heil Schicklegruber"?

DENNY

Oh, it's simple. But not that simple.

SOPHIE

It's not just to do what he wants about the articles?

DENNY

Sophie, I couldn't do that—though I love you from hell
to breakfast.

104

SOPHIE

There's no Munich for us, is there?

DENNY

No, not if we get out of here—
(*Off stage, in the hall, we hear the* CONSUL *engaged in argument with* MOE.)

CONSUL
(*Off stage—angrily*)
This happens every time—

MOE
(*Off stage*)
I'll send for the squad if the crowd gets bigger.
(*Enter the* CONSUL *from the hall.*)

SOPHIE

I can't help being terrified—

DENNY
(*Whispering*)
Heil Schicklegruber, remember—

SOPHIE

Mr. Denny, you are an astute observer of world events. Do you think Mr. Hitler will have another crisis this week-end?

DENNY

Yes, and if everybody can't come, he'll have it the next one.

CONSUL

(*With that charm which is going to make his sudden
demise inevitable*)
Everything happily arranged?


DENNY

Happily enough so you won't like it.


CONSUL

Sophie will tell me later. (*Turns on radio*) Sorry you are
leaving.

DENNY

Oh, I'm not. I've got a hunch this is the place to cover
this broadcast—

CONSUL

(*Shrugging*)
Well, the press is always welcome.


RADIO ANNOUNCER

. . . bringing you Chancellor Adolf Hitler on an international hookup from Nuremberg, Germany. Stand by, everybody. There's been a slight delay, caused by a sudden decision of the Fuehrer's not to broadcast, which he has since
changed—

DENNY

Ah! The Fuehrer's mind, working with its usual clarity.
(*There are now scattered shouts from the street. They
all turn toward the windows.*)


CONSUL

The voice of Democracy. Loud, but ineffectual.

106

DENNY

(*Going to window*)

That's what any donkey would say about thunder.

(HORST *bursts in from the office, breathless.*)


HORST

Baumer! Baumer! There's a mob in the street—


DENNY

A mob? A handful of picketers.


CONSUL

(*Indifferent*)

When the Fuehrer speaks, the dogs always gather to howl
at him out there. Baying at the moon, eh, Otto?


HORST

They may throw stink bombs!


DENNY

That wouldn't change this atmosphere much.


HORST

They must have followed *me*. They're calling for me.


CONSUL

Why don't you go out and drive them off?


HORST

(*At the window*)

Listen to what they're saying: "A tisket a tasket, put

Baumer in a casket." They mean *you!* You're the martyr they want, Baumer!

CONSUL

(*Happily*)

But I'm not the one they'll get.

HORST

(*Pointing to Hitler's bust, meaningfully*)

Now, Baumer, I warn you—I'd die for him, yes, but I'd *kill* for him, too!—I—

> (*Enter* MOE *quickly from hall. He goes at once to the alcove, starts to draw the curtains.*)

MOE

Listen, Mr. Baumer, I sent for the squad. You better draw them curtains— We're having a little trouble.

CONSUL

(*Fiercely*)

Stop that!

MOE

(*Stopping*)

But I'm telling you. Some of 'em is waving cucumbers and tomatoes. A couple of 'em is loaded with bricks. They might connect—

CONSUL

I am not afraid, Finkelstein. (*He goes to his desk, stands there in full view of the people in the street.*)

MOE

Say—them guys out there are mostly Wops and Polacks.

108

But our German citizens, which don't like no part of you or him, are what's getting out of hand now—

CONSUL

Get out!

MOE

(*Going to door*)

O.K. But if you stand in that window and get bopped by a seltzer bottle, I ain't gonna send no flowers to the hospital—

(*The* CONSUL *has picked the gun up from his desk. He has had one of his inspirations.*)

CONSUL

Finkelstein! You see this?

MOE

(*Turning*)

Yeah?

CONSUL

It's a gun. It's loaded. (*Looking at* DENNY) It was brought into this house by an uninvited guest.

DENNY

(*Laughing*)

Don't try a puerile trick like that, Baumer—

CONSUL

Horst, have I a witness?

HORST

Who? Me? Ah, absolutely!

CONSUL

It was used to threaten me.

MOE

You wanna prefer charges, sir?

CONSUL

Naturally. Finkelstein, you've allowed someone armed, without a permit, to enter my house. I am preferring charges against you—for dereliction of duty.

MOE

Aw—you can't do that, sir. It'd reflect on the whole force. Jeez, they'd *break* me—

CONSUL
*(Happily)*

I hope so.

MOE

Say, even you wouldn't do that to a family man. *(Pleading)* Listen, I got a *mother*. I got Momma's family. Listen, I'm in a jam like everybody else—

CONSUL

Horst, throw this fellow out!

HORST

Who, me?

MOE
*(Bitterly)*

A frameup, if I ever saw one! Listen, I'm a neutral and

I'm going to stay a neutral until I face you across a trench, and will I put six inches of steel right through your swastika—

CONSUL

Horst, thrash him.

HORST

(*Jittery*)

Baumer, you're the one he threatened!

MOE

(*To* HORST)

Listen, sweetheart, if you wanna fight, come around tomorrow morning, when I won't be wearing this uniform—

(*The* CONSUL *now sits at his desk, complacent, grinning, immobile, and turns his back on everyone, as if to listen in splendid isolation, to the radio.*)

RADIO ANNOUNCER

—there is still a delay in bringing you Chancellor Hitler.

DENNY

I hope it means somebody shot him.

MOE

From your mouth into God's ears, brother! (*Exits into hall.*)

RADIO ANNOUNCER

Your radio is not dead. Stand by, radio audiences—everywhere—

(*Enter* DR. JENNINGS *from the office, followed by* MAX. *The doctor is a bewildered and broken man.*)

III

DR. JENNINGS

Baumer! Herr Baumer—there is a mistake, some *terrible* mistake—

CONSUL

(*Impatiently as he rises from his desk*)

What is it, Doctor?

DR. JENNINGS

(*Agonized*)

His translation can't be correct—

CONSUL

(*Going to him*)

It says Norberg's free, doesn't it?

DR. JENNINGS

It says he's in a hospital, his mind completely gone—

CONSUL

He put it to rather bad use when he had it—

DR. JENNINGS

But it says my daughter—my *daughter* died in the camp—

SOPHIE

(*Going to him impulsively*)

Oh, Doctor, I'm so very, very sorry—

CONSUL

If you'd told me sooner she was your daughter—

DR. JENNINGS
(*Fiercely*)
You—you could have gotten her out long ago—


SOPHIE
Doctor, you *must* go home— (*She propels him gently to the door.*)

DR. JENNINGS
(*Crumpling*)
Yes, I must have self-control. I'll kill that man if I don't get out of here. (*Sobbing*) I'll kill him!


DENNY
(*To* CONSUL)
That makes three of us now who'd like to see you laid out with candles.

CONSUL
(*Not at all disturbed*)
The list is growing—
(SOPHIE *and* DR. JENNINGS *are now at the hall door.*)


SOPHIE
Officer! (*Enter* MOE) Get the doctor's car—


MOE
(*Firmly*)
I said it ain't healthy for *nobody* to leave the house. (*Exits, slamming the door in their faces.* SOPHIE *takes* DR. JENNINGS *to the big barrel-winged chair by the fireplace and presses him into it.*)

SOPHIE

Sit down for a moment, Doctor. Tom, get him a drink.
(DENNY *goes to the bar.*)

CONSUL

Doctor, we are all puppets of politics. Personally, my heart bleeds for you—

MAX

Sympathy from you?

CONSUL
(*Coldly*)
Please, Max. I've stood enough abuse for one day. Now, here's your letter.

SOPHIE

No! No! Max, don't read it—

MAX
(*In a thin, cold voice*)
I don't have to read it—

CONSUL
(*Opening it*)
Shall I read it *aloud* for you?

MAX

God damn you, no! (*He grabs the letter, and strides to the fireplace with it, glancing at it only for one agonized second before he throws it into the smoldering grate.* DR. JENNINGS, *his hand across his eyes, does not see him.* HORST, *who is still peeking at the street from behind the drapes at the window, looks back into the room for a moment, then drops down to the bar, pours himself a glass of beer, and, crouching in a corner, sips it nervously.)*

SOPHIE

Karl, he ought to kill you for that—

DENNY

That makes four, Baumer.

CONSUL

I am safe. I was born under the star of Hitler. You burned the letter, Max? Well, Schroeder has a photostatic copy—

MAX

*(Going to him)*

Gemeiner Schweinehund! You wanted witnesses. *(Agonized)* How could it help you to shatter my life to bits in front of *strangers?*

SOPHIE

Oh, Max, don't— *(She tries to put her arms around him. He twists away.)*

DENNY

But, man, you're in America now. That makes a difference—

SOPHIE

Yes, a lovely, lovely difference—

MAX

*(Whispering)*

Please leave me alone for a moment. *(He moves away from her to the middle of the room, too dazed to leave it.)*

CONSUL

My poor Max! (*He puts his arm consolingly around* MAX.)
How can they imagine what you must feel at this moment—

MAX

Don't touch me! (*He goes to the easy chair and falls into
it, sitting very still and white, staring with unseeing eyes into
a new and not very reassuring future.*)

CONSUL

(*Going to the bar*)
Oh, I don't mind. We are still in America— (*He pours a
glass of Scotch.*)

RADIO ANNOUNCER

We have now contacted Germany—

DENNY

Whenever two or three are gathered together in Hitler's
name, there is he also.

RADIO ANNOUNCER

—and we are turning you over to our Nuremberg announcer. (*Over the radio come the strains of a military band
playing "Deutschland über Alles," mingled with the bells of
Nuremberg.*)

CONSUL

I must have it quiet, please! (*He places the Scotch in front
of* MAX *on the low table at his elbow and returns to the bar
for his own drink.*)

116

RADIO ANNOUNCER

In the distance the lights of Old Nuremberg shine out, the *old* Germany—

CONSUL

(*Raising his glass*)

Which we reclaimed, like my *old* brandy—from a Rothschild cellar.

RADIO ANNOUNCER

—All at once the field is a blaze of floodlights. It is the signal. The Fuehrer has arrived!

(*The* CONSUL *goes to the bust of Hitler and raises his glass in a toast.*)

CONSUL

Der Fuehrer!

(*Simultaneously there is the blare of a motorcycle siren rounding a distant corner, and a well-aimed brick crashes through the window, missing the* CONSUL *so narrowly he staggers back to the table and puts his glass down.* HORST *fairly hops from his corner near the window and stands by the bar, quaking.* DENNY *goes to the window. Even* DR. JENNINGS *looks up for a moment, shaking his head as though this violent interruption were nevertheless part of the nightmare occurring in his brain.*)

DENNY

Well, that almost connected. }

*Together*

CONSUL

Where the hell is that policeman?

HORST

My God, they're throwing bricks—

*(There is the nearer howl of another police siren. The* CONSUL, *comforted, picks up glass.)*

RADIO ANNOUNCER

—We are waiting for the music to end, for Hitler to speak.

CONSUL

*(Laughing, as he stands on the alcove step, looking into the street.)*

And when Hitler speaks it is beautiful—such beautiful rhetoric!

DENNY

Be sure to let me know if he splits an infinitive before he splits up Poland.

CONSUL

Not a chance, Mr. Denny. *(Drinks)* Heil Hitler! *(A concert of shouts and sirens from under the window)* My Jewish Squad. I'll open the windows, so their Fuehrer can greet them. *(He goes behind the curtains.)*

RADIO ANNOUNCER

Hitler raises his arms. The music stops. Reichsfuehrer Adolf Hitler—! *(And now the Awful, Awful Voice of Hitler, the man who talked a nation and perhaps a civilization to its doom begins, hysterical, guttural, hideously sure and hard and loud. And at this exact moment the characters are thus disposed on the stage:* DENNY *standing in front of the fireplace,* DR. JENNINGS *slumped in the wing chair,* HORST *guzzling beer at the bar,* SOPHIE *leaning against the window,*

118

MAX, *rigid and white, his eyes closed, in the easy chair. After a few sharp beats of the* AWFUL VOICE, SOPHIE *turns and speaks to* DENNY. *We cannot hear her. But* DENNY *goes to her, puts his arm around her, and together they look out of the window, perhaps hoping on some misty horizon to see a better world.* HORST *chatters ecstatically to himself, bending over the bar, with a fresh beer glass. Now* MAX *rises, and impelled by the personal implications to himself of that radio voice, rushes to his office door. The* AWFUL VOICE *reaches an awful peroration— It is as if* MAX *heard it for the first time. He stops, horribly fascinated, and leans his averted face against the door frame. Then he goes and sits, huddled in the little chair by the window, half drawing the curtains around him in his misery. Now the* CONSUL, *still smiling happily, comes from behind the curtains. He looks at them all triumphantly, then sinks into his swivel chair, bent over his brandy glass, immobile, listening, his back to them all, as all theirs are to him now. His little Blitzkrieg has been enormously successful. Always the sedulous ape of his master, he now seems to be sunk in a deep Hitlerian silence, his swivel chair, in the raised alcove, is perhaps his Berchtesgaden—*HORST, *the other disciple, cocky in the reflected glory of* THE VOICE, *now falls contentedly into the easy chair* MAX *has vacated, putting his beer glass on the low table beside him. The* AWFUL VOICE *speaks about the Jews.* HORST, *hearing it, sets down his beer glass on the low table abruptly, and, rising on a sudden impulse, walks stealthily to the* CONSUL's *desk, reaches toward it, bending unseen around the back of the* CONSUL's *twisted chair. At this moment* DENNY *turns from the window to go to the bar. Quickly* HORST *drops down to the high table at the end of the settee, grabs a cigarette ostentatiously.* DENNY *sees him there, but turns back to the bar.* DR. JENNINGS *also looks up at* *him for a brief second, turns again to stare into the fireplace and* HORST, *looking oddly guilty, scuttles to the settee, and sits on the downstage end of it, hanging over the radio. Now* MAX *suddenly rises and goes to the desk. Cautiously, also, he approaches the* CONSUL's *back, reaching to the desk. The* CONSUL *half turns and his hand reaches out, as if to grab* MAX's. MAX *jerks back, moves away and then, like a man in a daze, falls once again into the easy chair, burying his face in his hands.* SOPHIE *turns to see* DENNY *at the bar, sees* MAX's *huddled shoulders, stoops over him to comfort him, changes her mind, and deliberately walks up to the* CONSUL. *She leans over him. The* AWFUL VOICE *rises again.* SOPHIE *pleads with the* CONSUL, *something perhaps he says causes her to stiffen, to sway, half drawing the curtain around her.* DENNY *at the bar, turns, sees her, goes to her at once. They both talk to the* CONSUL *in urgent voices that we cannot hear because of the radio. The* CONSUL *slowly, deliberately, moves the chair with its back to them, and turns his head away from them. The* AWFUL VOICE *goes on.*)

DENNY

(*To* CONSUL)

Well, my God, but isn't it loud enough! (*Taking* SOPHIE's *arm*) Sophie, we can't argue with a madman. (*He grabs her firmly by the arm, and guides her toward the sofa. There, they sit. No one has seen them. Suddenly* DENNY *raises his voice and shouts at* HORST) Hey, Horst! Baumer wants that louder! (*Obligingly* HORST *turns it up. And now the yammer gives way to the thunderous, sea-surge of the mob, the "Sieg Heil! Sieg Heil!"* SOPHIE *half rises.* DENNY *yanks her back.* DENNY's *mouth forms the word "Schicklegruber."* MAX *claps his hands over his ears. Now the maniacal roar of the "Sieg Heils" fills the theater.*)

(*Slowly, totally unperceived by anybody,* DR. JENNINGS *rises from his wing chair and walks to the* CONSUL'S *desk. Swiftly, deliberately, he whips the gun from the desk top and swiftly, deliberately, holds it around the chair to the* CONSUL'S *head and fires. The shot is lost in a last bestial howl from the radio. The* CONSUL'S *body falls abruptly forward, face down, on the desk.* DR. JENNINGS *turns, opens his mouth to speak. We cannot hear him. The gun in his outstretched hand, he moves forward to accuse himself. He speaks. Again we do not hear him. He looks up bewildered. He realizes they have not seen or heard. Then once again, he is in full possession of his faculties; he carefully wipes the handle of the gun on his coat, and carefully lays it by the right hand of the* CONSUL. *He then goes back to his wing chair. All that has been described here takes little more than two minutes on the stage. A second after* DR. JENNINGS *sinks into the chair, the hall door opens and* MOE *enters.*)

MOE
(*At the door, trying to shout down the radio*)
Hey! Mr. Baumer! Solomon's grabbed the guy which flung that brick. They got him at the station house. You wanna prefer charges?

HORST
(*Looking up*)
Sssh!

MOE
(*Going to the alcove*)
They gotta know. (*Bending over the* CONSUL) Listen, sir,

I said . . . *Jeez!* (*He sees that the man is dead. His first re-flex after that of surprise is a professional one. Quickly he inspects the windows of the alcove, the surface of the desk. Then he walks, his jaw set, to the steps of the alcove. He opens his mouth to shout the news to the occupants of the room, who are all sitting, their backs to him, with magnifi-cent dead-pans. Something about this inimical array of backs causes him to shut his mouth. And it is at that moment he re-members, what it may have seemed impossible he should ever forget, that he is a Jew, and that in this horrid circumstance he bears a curious responsibility. He whistles softly through his teeth and, wiping his forehead, looks Jehovahward im-ploringly as the curtain falls.*)

ACT TWO

# ACT TWO

*As the curtain rises, they are all in the same positions at
curtain of Act One.*

*The* AWFUL VOICE *is still screaming on.*

MOE *sets his jaw and claps his cap on his head with swift
decision. After a quick inspection of the windows, he comes
center stage and shouts to* HORST.

MOE

Turn that off! Turn that off!
> (HORST *looks up dumbfounded.* MOE *turns it off. Sur-
> prised, everyone looks at him.*)

HORST
*(Furious, half rising)*
What the devil do you mean by this?

MOE
*(Pointing a threatening finger at him)*
Don't move!

DENNY
*(Laughing, half rising)*
So Baumer's fed up. God knows I am.

MOE
*(Points threateningly at him also)*
Don't move. None of you.

HORST
*(Rises)*

Herr Baumer—

MOE
*(Thrusting him back on settee)*
Listen! He ain't gonna answer. Ever. Baumer is—dead.
*(There is a silence. Oddly enough, no one seems to react to
this staggering information at all)* Sa-ay, that's a *terrific* bomb-
shell, in case you folks don't know it!

HORST
*(Whispering)*
Are you *sure* he's dead?

MOE
Yeah, Otto. An autopsy's the only future Mr. Baumer's got.

DR. JENNINGS
*(Rising, the efficient physician in an emergency and
moving to alcove)*
Probably a thrombosis.

MOE
*(Stopping him)*
Don't move. This wasn't no thrombis. Not if that's some-
thing natural.

DR. JENNINGS
*(Brightly appalled)*
*Suicide?*

126

DENNY
*(Stunned)*

He shot himself?

HORST

Yes! He *shot* himself! *(Rising, rapturously)* O God, the courage, the beautiful courage!

MOE
*(Suspiciously)*
How do *you* know he shot himself?

HORST

Because— *(Slyly as he sinks back on the settee)* Ha! I don't know it. I don't know *anything*.

MOE

Anybody hear a shot?

DR. JENNINGS
The radio must have drowned it. . . .

DENNY
The radio was going full blast. . . .

HORST
The radio—the Sieg Heils on the radio . . .     } *Together*

SOPHIE
You couldn't hear anything with the radio . . .

MAX
The radio—the Fuehrer was speaking. . . .

127

DR. JENNINGS
(*Going to* MOE)
Officer, this place has been a bedlam for the last three minutes. At least, *I* heard nothing.

MAX
(*Rises*)
But why would Baumer commit suicide—unless—

MOE
(*Sharply*)
Unless *what?*

DR. JENNINGS
(*Reasonably*)
Unless he had some reason— (*Quietly*) which I naturally wouldn't know about.

DENNY
(*Eagerly*)
He had a damned good reason. He'd been a failure—

SOPHIE
(*Enthusiastically*)
Yes, I can explain, Officer. He'd been taking Nazi funds.

MAX
Yes. To play the market.

HORST
(*Rising, indignant*)
Ridiculous! Libeling the *dead!*

128

SOPHIE

No. And he'd been recalled to Germany. That's true, Max,
isn't it?

MAX

Yes. The orders from Berlin are in that desk. (*He moves
to desk.* MOE *stops him.*)

MOE

Now get this fast, everybody! This wasn't no suicide. This
was—murder!

ALL

Murder!

HORST

Absolutely! Ha! This was murder!

MOE

(*Confronts* HORST)

How do *you* know it's murder? A second ago you knows
it's suicide. Why'd you change your mind so sudden?

HORST

(*Cunningly*)

I was merely echoing your remark. You seem so very sure
of yourself.

DENNY

(*To* SOPHIE, *who has turned her white face away from
the still, slumped figure in the swivel chair*)
Go to your room.

MOE

(*Fiercely*)

None of you is leaving!

DENNY

But can't you see how this is for Mrs. Baumer!

MOE

I can see this guy's been bumped off, and one of you is
guilty.

HORST
(*Sneering*)

Yes, *one* of us is guilty.

DR. JENNINGS
(*Very reasonably*)

But that's impossible. We were all sitting here quietly listening to the radio. Somebody must have come through the
window. The last thing we heard him say was that he was
going to open the window.

MAX

Then somebody from the street must have climbed through
the window.

MOE

But nobody didn't. Because the window is locked inside.
How do you like that?

DENNY

But they may have shot him through it?

MOE

No. There ain't no holes in the window. The only hole's
in him. (SOPHIE *exclaims in dismay at this too lucid piece of
information*) I'm sorry, lady. (*Tactfully he closes the alcove*

*curtains. That is the last we see of Herr Consul Baumer.*
MOE *goes quietly to the door, right*) Where's that door go to?
(*Opens it.*)

MAX

To the bedrooms.

MOE

Does the help's quarters join 'em?

MAX

No.

SOPHIE

Oh, there's no one in there now. The servants have to come
through the hall.
(MOE *closes the door.*)

MAX

They're in the kitchen now, listening to the radio.

DR. JENNINGS
(*Going toward hall*)

I'll get them.

MAX
(*Following him*)

Let me. They speak only German.

MOE
(*Savagely*)

They can stay in the kitchen.

DR. JENNINGS

But surely you should question them?

MOE

They can't tell me nothing I want to know. Because I was in that hall the whole time. Nobody could come in that way without me seeing them. And nobody didn't. Get it?

HORST

(*Delighted*)

Exactly. Nobody did come in that way—but the officer.

MOE

Stop stooging for me, Otto. It makes me nervous.

DR. JENNINGS

(*Incredulous*)

Officer, are you implying that only one of us could have done it?

MOE

*Now* you're tuned in!

DENNY

You're actually accusing one of us? That's a strong accusation.

MOE

(*Tight-lipped*)

I'm making it.

HORST

The best defense is a strong attack. Ha!

MOE

(*Urgently*)

Now if the guy who done it will come clean, I'll call **for**

the Homicide, and the rest of you can go about your business.
(*Moves expectantly to telephone. A pause.*)

DR. JENNINGS

Well, we're naturally shocked, but none of us is behaving
at all like a man with a murder on his conscience.

MOE

Listen, I ain't no Sherlock Holmes, but the party, or parties,
that did this pulled one boner.

DR. JENNINGS

He left a clue perhaps? (*Feeling his own breast pocket as
he talks*) He dropped a handkerchief, a fountain pen—

MOE

I ain't saying what it is. But any dope would know it spelt
murder.

DENNY

Then you'd better call the Homicide now. You're not in
a position to investigate this alleged crime. If it's not suicide,
there's some simple explanation of how the criminal got in.

MAX

A trained mind will find it.

DENNY

By this delay you may be helping a dangerous criminal in
making his getaway.

DR. JENNINGS

Precisely.

133

MAX

Officer, I agree with these gentlemen.

HORST

But I agree with the officer! (*He confronts* MOE, *his nostrils twitching with excitement*) Yes, one of us in this room is a mad dog, a killer! Proceed, Finkelstein. It's interesting to see your mind work.

MOE

Listen, Otto, if my mind can't work now, I may as well swop it for yours, God forbid . . . Look, everybody, *I'm* in a very unusual situation—

DR. JENNINGS

The Chinese say a wise man never finds a dead one.

MOE

I wish to hell this had all happened in China.

DENNY

(*Going to telephone*)

If you won't phone for the Homicide, I will!

MOE

For God's sake, Mister, wait! (*With bitter urgency*) *I* was responsible for that guy's safety.

DR. JENNINGS

(*Puzzled*)

No one can hold you responsible for what happened in this room, if you were not in it.

134

HORST

*If* he was not in it! Ha!

MOE

*My name is Moe Finkelstein.*

HORST

Exactly!

DENNY

Don't get the connection—

DR. JENNINGS

Nor I.

MOE
(*Points to* HORST)

He got it. Right away *he* got it!

MAX
(*Dully*)

Yes—and I think I get it, too.

SOPHIE

But *you* had no motive—

MOE

Lady, for a lot of people, the shape of my nose is *plenty* of motive.

DENNY
(*Indignantly*)

But hell, man, you're in America!

135

MOE

Likewise I'm an American. So I ain't worried much about myself. But there's still a lot of people with noses like mine in Germany. Look, the squad gets here, and reporters—and there ain't nobody obliging 'em with no snap confession. So coroner's inquests take hours. (*Looks at* HORST) But cables to Germany go fast!

MAX
(*Sharply*)

I remember what happened in Berlin when Grynszpan shot the Secretary of our Paris Embassy.

(*There is a pause, they all look at one another like people caught in a shameful unwilling conspiracy.*)

DR. JENNINGS
(*Decisively*)

Yes. *You* need an alibi. I can give you one. (*Pointing to his armchair*) I was sitting in that chair from the time the Consul went to his desk alive. After that I saw you come into this room only *once.*

MOE
(*Looking at his watch*)

Five minutes ago, by the hall door?

DR. JENNINGS

Precisely.

HORST
(*In a dither of excitement to* DR. JENNINGS)

Ah, but suppose he had tiptoed in by the office door, behind you?

MOE

Yeah, Doc. I coulda done that?


HORST

(*Jumps forward and puts his face close to* MOE'S)
You did do it. I saw you!


MOE

(*Contemptuously*)
You saw me plug your boss? If you didn't make a stink,
you're an accessory, you dope!


HORST

Hum . . . But! You don't deny you *could* have come in
that way unperceived by all of us, including the doctor?


MOE

Nope. I gotta admit that one.


HORST

Exactly! You sneaked in with revenge and murder in your
heart—

MOE

In one minute you'll make me so sore I'll say I done it
and bump you off next!

HORST

(*Triumphantly*)
A double confession!

MOE

(*Turning to the others sadly*)
So! This ain't Germany. This is *America*. And look at the

137

spot I'm in already. Jeez, you gotta help me. I ain't asking it
for myself—

MAX

He's asking it for a hundred thousand innocent people he
never laid eyes on.

MOE

(*Puzzled*)

Say, you're a funny kind of a Heinie.

MAX

(*In a flat voice*)

Yes, I'm a funny kind of a Heinie.

DR. JENNINGS

Now look here. Murder isn't pretty. And I'm not sure even
now that it's ever justifiable—

MOE

(*Suspiciously*)

What do you mean—even *now?*

DR. JENNINGS

I mean, Baumer was a man who invited murder. But if you
murder a man, you usually swing for it. No sane man would
care to swing for killing a hyena like Baumer. I wouldn't.
But I'm innocent, so I'm willing to help you get an alibi.
(*Looking down his glasses at* HORST) In fact, anyone who
refused to help would create the impression in my mind that
*he* was the guilty one.

SOPHIE

Oh, Officer, there's no use in going through this—(DENNY

*quickly thrusts her down into the easy chair and stands protectingly over her.)*

DENNY

(*Gently*)

Sophie, all the boy needs is an *alibi*. Won't you help him?

MAX

I'll help. Officer, it's perfectly apparent to me that you are entirely innocent.

MOE

(*Sarcastic*)

Well, that's damned white of you.

HORST

(*Exasperated*)

Innocent? What is the matter with all you Dummkopfs? He had a quarrel with Baumer. We all heard him. He threatened to kill him. You probably destroyed the real evidence against you just now when you went behind that curtain. But the evidence that you can't destroy is that you had a motive and absolutely no alibi—unless you can make one of these blind fools give it to you.

DR. JENNINGS

Horst, you're deliberately trying to pin this thing on this boy!

HORST

But obviously. We are Aryans. Why, if he's not guilty, then one of us is. That would be a pretty kettle of gefüllte fish!

139

MOE

Listen, folks, this guy is going to bust any alibi you can hand me. So I'm gonna need more'n a alibi. I'm gonna need the murderer.

DENNY
(*Moving up on him*)
Horst! Suppose I said: I know you did it!

HORST

Who? Me? Did you see me? (*Triumphantly*) Then you're an accessory, you dope!

DENNY

If this is going to be a game of pinning on the donkey's tail, Fuehrer Horst, you're my candidate!

DR. JENNINGS
(*Also moving up on him*)
And mine. Swinging *you* for this would be a public service.

SOPHIE
(*Grimly*)

Bravo, Doctor!

MOE
(*His spirits rising*)
Say! I gotta admit this is unexpected co-operation.

DR. JENNINGS

Not at all, my boy. It will be a pleasure. Now, how do we proceed, Officer?

MOE

First, I'd like to ask a coupla questions. Anybody without

a murder on his conscience won't find no trouble answering
them.

HORST

I say nothing until I consult my lawyer, Benjamin Rosenblatt.

DENNY

Exactly the tone a guilty man takes.


HORST

I know my legal rights. This is entirely irregular! I want
to get out of here! (*He makes a swift move to the door.*
DENNY *collars him.*)

DENNY

(*Shaking him*)
We could begin with a little third degree—


MOE

Don't bother. The Homicide Squad will take care of that.
They'll massage him with a hose. He'll come out a couple of
inches shorter. Otto, you'll do yourself a favor if you let me
operate. (HORST *sinks into the easy chair, unhappy but con-
vinced.*)

HORST

Baron, you're in charge of this Consulate now. How can
you let this foreigner bulldoze us?


MAX

But if you are not guilty, Horst? I am willing to answer
all his questions.

HORST

But remember anything you say can be used against you.

MOE

That's right, folks. But what can you lose? You can prac-
tice your answers on me—for Mulrooney.

HORST

Mulrooney?

MOE

Captain of the Homicide. And, boy, when Mulrooney asks
questions, you think he's your conscience talking.

HORST
(*Sagely*)
I'll still take my chances with the Irish.

MOE
(*Confidentially*)
Listen, you wanna make a deal?

HORST

A deal?

MOE

Just stick around. And when the reporters and cameramen
get here, I let *you* take over the spotlight cold and hand them
the murderer.

HORST
(*Rises and comes towards* MOE)
You're just challenging me to pit my brains against yours,
aren't you?

MOE

Yeah. (*Humbly*) And for you a poor schnuckle like me
ought to be a pushover.

**HORST**
*(Swaggering)*
It's a deal. Proceed, Officer.


**MOE**
*(Confronting them all)*
Look. I don't know about *you* guys, but this is *my* first murder. I'm just an ordinary flatfoot. But I go to the movies. When it's a murder dish, the first thing you gotta get is motives. O.K. Motives!

**HORST**
You had the only motive!


**DR. JENNINGS**
Oh, no. I had quite a good one.


**SOPHIE**
Don't—don't talk like that, Doctor!


**DR. JENNINGS**
My dear child, all these things must come out at the inquest— Officer, I often came here to see the Consul. He was trying to get my son-in-law and my daughter out of a concentration camp. Rather, I believed he was trying. About an hour ago I learned that she had died there—


**MAX**
I'll verify that.

**HORST**
Why didn't you go home after the bad news? No one invited you to stay!

MOE

I invited him. I told him it wasn't healthy to leave. (*Slaps himself on the head*) Finkelstein keeping people out of trouble!

HORST

(*Thrilled with his own shrewdness*)
Exactly. He just sat in that chair, plotting! When the Heil Hitlers came on, he crept to Baumer's desk—

MOE

Did *you* see him?

HORST

No. (*Ecstatic*) But it stands to reason— Look at the layout of this room, think where you found us! He's the only one who could have moved without being seen by the rest of us!

MOE

Otto, control your convulsions. Nobody saw nobody commit no murder, or they'd have hollered like hell for a copper.

HORST

Um—unless somebody is protecting somebody else!

MOE

That's why I'm doing motives, dope! Mr. Denny—you got a motive?

DENNY

Yes. I'm in love with Mrs. Baumer, and she's in love with me.

SOPHIE
(*Taking* DENNY's *hand*)
Oh, terribly. And my husband knew it.


MOE
Sa-ay! Prying loose incriminating evidence like this takes months in front of a jury.


DENNY
But eventually it would be pried. And we want to see justice done— (*Glowering at* HORST) quickly!


MOE
Jeez, you people are the salt of the earth. In a minute I'll bust out crying. So what about you, Baron. Got a motive?


MAX
I? I was his closest friend in America. No. No, I had no motive.

MOE
(*To all*)
Check?

DR. JENNINGS
I know of none. (*Coldly*) But the Baron was and is in a state of hyper-tension. Frankly, the Baron would be my second candidate.

SOPHIE
(*Quickly*)
Oh, no, Doctor! I know him very well, Officer. The Baron is a loyal Nazi.

MOE

You check that, Mr. Denny?


DENNY

(*Reluctantly*)

I'll take Sophie's word for it.


MOE

O.K. Now, Otto, *you* can rattle your tonsils. What've you got to say for yourself?

HORST

(*Loftily*)

No motive.

DENNY

He must have a motive. Sooner or later Baumer would supply a motive to anybody who worked with him, gratis.


DR. JENNINGS

I'm sure of it. As Professor Norberg put it in his study of Criminality, the solution of any crime lies in the personality of the murdered man himself.


DENNY

Add, that Horst *looks* like a killer.


DR. JENNINGS

(*Eyeing* HORST *critically*)

I see your point. The occipital lobes *are* rather enlarged. The receding brow, the projecting ears. He does look like a killer.

146

HORST

So you democrats don't approve of persecution! I suppose *I'm* not being persecuted! Why, you're trying to make a political martyr of me. (*Teetering on his heels in an excess of self-confidence*) Well, that time's past.

MOE

What do you mean by that, Otto?

HORST

I mean that a Jew killed him instead of me, the more logical victim.

MAX
(*Disgusted*)

Oh, I wouldn't be surprised, Horst, if I could find you a motive.

HORST

Look here, Baron. Are you for me or against me? I haven't breathed a word about *your* possible motives.

MAX
(*Nervously*)

I'm not against you, Horst. I just feel that we all ought to admit anything that might have any *direct* bearing on the murder. (*Lamely*) I'm for you, really.

HORST

Then I'm for you, Baron. (*He bows.*)

MOE

Lucky you two guys met. Aw, you're both stalling!

147

**HORST**

You're egging us on against each other. Oh, the Judaic mind! And that's what Aryan must fight Aryan for in Europe. (*Goes to* MOE) You egg us on and then duck while civilization perishes!

**MOE**

Now just for that, Otto, I'm going to have Momma put the curse on you. (HORST *laughs*) Don't laugh, Otto. You don't know Momma— O.K. These three got motives . . . (*To* HORST *and* MAX) And you two palookas ain't coming clean yet. (*Abruptly*) So who owned the weapon?

**HORST**

Ha! He showed the gun to you!

**DENNY**

To all of us.

**DR. JENNINGS**

And we all knew it was loaded.

**MOE**

But who brought it in here, I'm asking?

**HORST**

Denny did. Baumer said he was going to prefer charges.

**MOE**

All guns carry serial numbers. It's gonna be easy to trace where it was bought.

148

HORST

Not where I bought this one!
(*They all laugh in spite of themselves.*)

MAX

Dummkopf!

HORST
(*Hysterically*)
You trapped me! Why, this—this is encirclement!

MOE
(*Wearily*)
I'm a sap to waste Momma's curse on a schlemiel like Otto.
Otto, how come the Consul had your gun?

HORST

He took it away from me this afternoon. (*Petulantly*) I had
no permit.

DENNY

Make a note of that.

MOE

That should slip my mind? Don't worry. O.K. That gets
the gun out of the way.

DENNY

Won't there be fingerprints on it?

MOE

I ain't expecting any.

DR. JENNINGS

You mean somebody wiped them off?

149

MOE

(*To* HORST)

Ain't that what you'd do if you was a murderer?

HORST

Yes, surely. I mean—no. (*Furiously*) Stop trying to trap me!

MOE

O.K. Now, folks, we got a weapon. Likewise all the motives we'll get till this brace of goose-steppers starts squealing. (*To* HORST *and* MAX) Now let's straighten out the chronic of events leading up to this murder.

DENNY

Well, it all began in 1923 with a beer-hall putsch in Munich.

MOE

I get you. But if we start going back that far, we're sure to wind up in the Garden of Eden, cross-examining the snake. O.K. We'll begin with the putsch at 5:07 o'clock on this block.

HORST

Why?

MOE

On account of at that hour we was all in this room. And one of us had the opportunity for murder some time after that. So it's 5:07 o'clock, and in I breezes, and tells Baumer he's gotta close them drapes or he's gonna get conked. (*Shrugging*) And was Finkelstein a prophet! So Baumer tells me to scram, and I makes a mellerdramatic exit—

**HORST**

Vowing vengeance on Baumer.

**MOE**

Nope. I just wished him he should grow like a onion, with his head in the ground forever. Which is nothing compared to what Momma's going to wish Otto. O.K. Exit copper— enter brick. That's one minute later—5:08 o'clock.

**HORST**

How do you know?

**MOE**

`I referred to my watch.

**HORST**

You seem to refer to your watch quite frequently.

**MOE**

So what do you do with yours, take your pulse? Now, Mr. Denny, when that rock comes in, is the Consul at his desk?

**DENNY**

*(Before the bust of Hitler)*

No. He was standing right here with his drink, toasting Hitler.

**MOE**

O.K. So he toasted the bust. Then what?

**DENNY**

Well, the brick almost hit him. There was a second of natural confusion. Then the Consul went to those steps.

151

**HORST**

Yes, I remember. Just as Hitler began to speak.

**MOE**

5:10 o'clock.

**DENNY**

Then he heiled Hitler, gave us a little Nazi sales talk—and said he was going to open the windows.

**MOE**

Why'd he want to open the windows?

**DENNY**

So your boys in the street could have the benefit of Hitler's message.

**MOE**

Big-hearted Baumer.

**DR. JENNINGS**

The last thing we heard him say was that he was going to open the window. Officer, are you sure the windows—?

**MOE**

Let me worry, Doc. I come from a long line of worriers. Then what did Baumer do after that?

**DENNY**

Well, Baumer went behind the curtain. After that—I guess we all sat down to listen to the radio.

152

MOE

Now did anybody see Baumer come back and sit down?

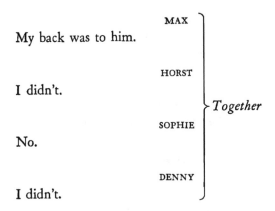

MAX

My back was to him.

HORST

I didn't.

Together

SOPHIE

No.

DENNY

I didn't.

DR. JENNINGS

From my chair, I could see everything but the Consul.

MOE

So nobody actually saw him sit?

HORST

You say *you* found him sitting. Maybe that's suspicious!

MOE

Yeah! Maybe I met him in the men's room where I drills him and then drags him back and props him up—lifesize. O.K. So that means you all must have gone to sit down while Baumer was letting the hot air out?

DENNY

I suppose it does—yes.

153

MOE

Now, Doc, where was you when the Consul heiled Hitler?


DR. JENNINGS

I was sitting in this chair. (*He sits in his wing chair.*)


MOE

Mr. Denny?

DENNY

I was over there. (*Goes to the mantelpiece.*)


MOE

Baron?

MAX

I was here (*Indicating his Scotch*), with the drink he poured me. (*He sits in the easy chair.*)


MOE

Mrs. Baumer?

SOPHIE
(*Goes to window*)
I was here, by the window.


MOE

Horst?

HORST
(*Goes to bar*)
Here, drinking my pale Hofbrau.


MOE

Doc, you check that?

154

DR. JENNINGS

(*Considers for a moment*)

Well, yes—

MOE

Everybody check?

ALL

(*Dubiously—eyeing one another, yet giving and getting unspoken mutual corroboration*)
Yes— Guess so— Didn't notice— Yes—

MOE

O.K., folks, stay like that. (*Goes to alcove steps, removes his coat and hat and hangs them on the railing*) Because now we're going to do opportunities, which you all had from the time the Consul comes to these steps.

DENNY

(*Uneasily*)
Officer, I hope you're using some kind of a system.

MOE

Yeah. From here out, I use the Braille system. Now, lady, with your kind permission I'm going to impersonate your dear, departed husband . . . Momma should see me— O.K. (*On step, striking a stance*) So I'm Baumer, and I says "Heil Hitler!" (*Salutes, raises his eyes to ceiling*) God forgive me! And Hitler's a great guy, and he's gonna mop up the world, and baloney and baloney and baloney, and people ain't got enough on their minds, so I'll just open the windows for it. (*Half steps behind the curtain*) Now go and park yourselves where you went after I said that— (SOPHIE *sits down on sofa at right*. DENNY *goes directly to sit with* SOPHIE. HORST *sits on*

155

*settee left. Neither the* DOCTOR *or* MAX *needs to move.* MOE *looks at them critically*) Say! This is exactly the way I found you when I come in by the hall door and stumbles across the stiff.

HORST

Ha! Exactly. Why not?

DR. JENNINGS
(*Worried*)

Officer, if you were on duty in the hall, can't Officer Solomon give you an alibi?

MOE

Sol took the German who tossed the confetti through the window to the station house. When that brick came in, my alibi went out. How many minutes do you figure you was like this before I makes my entrance?

DENNY

Well, with the radio—

SOPHIE

Hitler was speaking—

MAX

He was going on and on and on—   *Together*

HORST

When our Fuehrer speaks, time has no meaning.

DR. JENNINGS

Well, possibly a minute.

156

MOE

(*Going quickly to* DR. JENNINGS)

A minute, from when *you* sat down there, Doc?

(*A pause.* DR. JENNINGS *bites his lip.*)

DR. JENNINGS

Oh, it may have been a minute, an hour, or an eternity. . . .

MOE

The speech went on at 5:10. (*To* HORST) I looked at my watch. It's now 5:33. We been at this twenty minutes.

HORST

Getting nowhere!

MOE

Thanks for pacing me. So *you* sat down in that chair, Doc, just one minute before I come in from the hall and finds the corpse?

DR. JENNINGS

(*Uneasily*)

I'm not a very good judge of time.

MOE

Most doctors is. So you say you sat down at five-*twelve*?

DR. JENNINGS

No. No. It must have been before that.

SOPHIE

(*Helpfully*)

Oh, it was before that. Doctor, you sat down long before Hitler began?

DR. JENNINGS
Yes. I was so stunned, I must have lost track of time.


MOE
But if you sat down before Hitler started to speak—then you was already sitting at 5:12. Closer to half an hour than one minute?

DR. JENNINGS
Yes. Closer to half an hour. Yes.


MOE
Um . . . (*He eyes the doctor thoughtfully, then suddenly seems to dismiss his own reflections with a shrug*) Now, Doc, *after* everybody was in these positions, nobody moved at no time?

DR. JENNINGS
Afterwards, Officer, nobody. But before—while Hitler was speaking . . . (*Nervously*) You *must* let me think.


MOE
Sure, Doc. (*Gently*) Think hard what you were doing for the *other* twenty-nine minutes. Now, are all the rest of you sure, after you sat in these positions, nobody moved at no time?

HORST
How many times must we reiterate? Nobody!


MOE
(*Wearily*)
Which, if nobody is lying, proves *I* must of come in by the office door and done it!

158

**HORST**

Is that your confession?

**MOE**

*(Angrily)*

No, that's just your theory.

**DR. JENNINGS**

But one of us *is* lying. That's obvious. *(Rises)* Now I must help. I was sitting in this chair, where you must realize I was in a unique position to commit this murder.

**MOE**

Yeah. I realize it.

**DR. JENNINGS**

But I didn't do it!

**MOE**

*(Leans over the doctor and says kindly)*

Doc, you look like a good guy. If you say you didn't, I'll try to believe you.

**DR. JENNINGS**

Thank you. But I was also in a unique position to see the actions of everyone else in this room.

**HORST**

If you saw all of us, we all have alibis now. You said in the beginning none of us moved.

**DR. JENNINGS**

No, Horst. I said none of you moved *after* we were all in

the positions in which the officer found us. But before—while Hitler was speaking—

MOE

Now take it easy, Doc. Folks, I wanna make a announcement. (*He turns to the others*) After you all heard Baumer say he was gonna open the window, one of you did move. Now how do I know that? Because I was in the hall when you turned up the radio. After Hitler turns the juice on, I went into the Baron's office—

HORST

Why?

MOE
(*Patiently*)

Otto, them Heil Hitlers don't relax me. Now, when I was in the office, I looked through that door once. (*Points to open office door*) And I saw somebody in here moving.

ALL

Who?

MOE

I ain't saying who yet.

HORST
(*Nervously*)

You mean the person you saw moving is the one you're going to accuse of murder?

MOE

I'm saying, any guy who ain't willing to admit he got an attack of wanderlust during that speech is a pretty suspicious

160

character. And will the D.A. get a load of it. O.K. Now everybody go back to the Heil Hitler positions.

(*They all return to the same positions as the beginning of the previous re-enactment.*)

DR. JENNINGS

I was sitting in this chair—

MOE

(*On the alcove steps*)

Doc, you was sitting in that chair *much* longer than you think. Now I'm the Consul again. Heil Hitler—

HORST

(*Saluting automatically*)

Heil Hitler!

MOE

You're a self-starter, ain't you? Now, I'm the Consul again. Heil Hitler and— Blah, blah, blah, and I'm gonna open the windows. (*He takes a half step back and bumps accidentally against the concealed swivel chair. Turns toward it*) Please excuse me! (*To the others*) Now, get going. (SOPHIE *and* DENNY *sit on sofa at right, as previously.* MAX *still doesn't move. But now instead of going directly to the settee,* HORST *goes to the easy chair.*)

HORST

(*Pointing at chair*)

Here. That's where *I* went.

MAX

No. Here's my whiskey.

HORST
(*Pointing to his own glass*)
And my pale Hofbrau.

MAX
(*Angrily*)
You're trying to prove I moved!

HORST
I'm admitting I did.

MAX
Yes, but not at my expense!

HORST
Baron, your whole attitude throughout has been traitorous
to Germany and to me— (*Very significantly*) but I can guess
why! (MAX *rises quickly and* HORST *plumps himself into his
vacated chair and relaxes luxuriantly.*)

MOE
You want your pipe and evening paper?

SOPHIE
Max, isn't there any fight in you?

MAX
(*Standing near Hitler bust*)
Sophie, I'm also in an unusual situation.

MOE
(*Grimly*)
Now, Otto! First you said you was sitting there. (*Points to*

*the settee*) Now you say it's here. So when did you go there (*Points to settee*) where I found you?

HORST

I just walked there, a few seconds later. Like this— (*Rises and is about to cross downstage directly.*)

DR. JENNINGS<br>(Shouting)

No, Horst! You never crossed like that! Officer, now I remember clearly. I did see Horst get up, and as I recollect, rather stealthily—

DENNY<br>(Delighted at the unexpected success of MOE's peripatetic method of detection)

Now we're getting somewhere, Officer.

HORST<br>(Comes toward DR. JENNINGS)

How could you see me?

DR. JENNINGS<br>(Pointing at his eye)

Out of the tail of my eye, Fuehrer.

HORST

You said you couldn't see the desk!

DR. JENNINGS<br>(Rises)

No. But you came that way— (*Indicating an upstage cross to desk.*)

163

MOE

Can anybody else check that Otto came that way?


DENNY

Yes, I can. I didn't see Horst get up. But—well—as a matter of fact, I was over here by the bar and—


MOE

Anhanh! So *you* started circulating?


DENNY

Yes. I turned and saw Horst leaving the desk, looking damned green about the gills—


HORST

That's a lie! I didn't go near the desk. I came directly here for a cigarette.

DR. JENNINGS

No, Horst. If you'd come directly here, I'd have seen you the whole time. As it was—you passed out of my range of vision, for at least one minute.


MOE

Yeah, you could have done it in a minute.


HORST

(*Gibbering*)

Look, if I was prowling around like that, where was the Baron? He said first he was in that chair. But I was. Ask him where he went before *I* got up!

164

MAX

Never mind, Horst. I did get up from that chair before Horst sat down. I intended to leave the room, but I—just stood in the office door. (*He does so now to demonstrate it.*)

MOE

Thanks. That's what I was coming to. Because that's what I saw from the office. I saw you, standing there. Why was you standing there?

MAX

Something Hitler said caught my attention.

MOE

It must have been something awful sad. From where I was you looked like you was bawling.

MAX

I had just received a letter from Berlin, that my little sister was very ill there.

HORST

That's a strange kind of a letter to burn, Baron!

MAX

(*Angrily*)

I burned the letter because— (*Then controlling himself*) one's first reaction to sorrow is often anger.

SOPHIE

Officer, the Baron's family troubles have nothing to do with this investigation!

165

HORST
(*Slyly*)
Don't be too sure of that, Mrs. Baumer!


MOE
What do you mean by that?


HORST
For the moment I'll hold my tongue.


MOE
So you've got your hands full. (*To* MAX) O.K., you stood in the door. Then what?

MAX
Then I sat in this little chair, for a minute perhaps— (*Sits down on chair under window*) Then I came over here like this—to get my drink— (*Rises—and goes to easy chair*) This is where you found me. (*Sits.*)


MOE
At which point, where was old blowhole?


MAX
Otto? (*Smiling*) At the radio.
    (HORST *sits down on settee, bending triumphantly over radio.*)

MOE
But while you was playing puss-in-the-corner, you didn't see Otto go near the desk?

166

MAX

No.

MOE

But you could have?

MAX

I could have, of course. But I guess I closed my eyes.

MOE

On purpose?

MAX

No, Officer. I closed them to look at other things.

MOE
(*Bewildered*)
You closed your eyes to look at other things?

MAX

Things that have happened down the centuries.

MOE

Doc, you better watch this guy. He's a little screwy. Now, Doc, where does that leave us?

DR. JENNINGS
(*Firmly*)
It leaves Horst with a fine opportunity to commit murder.

MOE

Yeah, Doc. But it's all circumstantial. You can't fry a guy for stretching his legs while Hitler is speaking. Anyway, not in this country.

167

HORST

Exactly! And after I sat down here I never moved! I know, because that's when Hitler said— (*Shrilly*) Oh, my God! I've got my alibi! (*He grabs his head with wild exuberance*) That's when I turned the radio up louder. I turned it up when he said— (*Looking at* DENNY) No, when he said— (*Looking at alcove.*)

MOE

(*Putting his arm on* HORST's *shoulder*)
When *who* said?

HORST

When *Baumer* said, "Turn it up louder!" You both know that's true. You heard it!

MOE

Lady, did you hear your husband tell Otto to turn the radio up louder?

SOPHIE

Yes, I did! Oh— (*Breaking down*) Tom, I *can't*—

DENNY

Heil Schicklegruber!

SOPHIE

No. I've got to tell him. I can't play this ugly game any longer.

DENNY

(*Going quickly to* MOE)
Then *I'll* tell it. I was at the bar. Mrs. Baumer was there by the window. I looked around and saw her going to Baumer's desk.

MOE

(*Pointing to radio*)

After Otto was there?

SOPHIE

Yes. Yes. I went to my husband because I meant to—

DENNY

Shut up! I'm telling this. So I went right after her. She started to argue with Baumer. I told her it was useless, the man was a maniac. He said: "Turn the radio up louder."

HORST

Yes. So I did it! Like this— (*He turns on the radio. Surprise, surprise, Hitler is still speaking. . . . With infinite disgust* MOE *turns it off.*)

MOE

(*As he clicks it off*)

Coming to you by courtesy of David Sarnoff— O.K. Now where are we? After Baumer went to his desk, the doctor never moved at no time. The Baron here moved first. He could have done it. Otto moved next. Otto could have done it. Then Mrs. Baumer and Mr. Denny goes to the desk. But when they was up there, Baumer was still living because he tells them to turn the radio up louder. And then they both goes and parks themselves on that sofa. After that the Doc says nobody moved. O.K. So everybody but me and the Doc has got alibis. Maybe they ain't good ones, but all everybody's gotta do is stick to them. Because there ain't no witnesses. Nobody saw nobody commit no murder. It's the perfect crime, folks. Which leaves me where I started—the perfect scapegoat. (*Wearily*) I guess I never had much of a chance

169

to unravel this one. I kinda hoped if the guy who done it had any sense of justice—which leaves you out, Otto—he'd say so. But I got too much faith in human nature. O.K. So there ain't nothing much going to happen to me. But a lot of innocent people is going for a hell of a bloody sleigh-ride— (*Walks to the phone and starts to dial.*)


DR. JENNINGS
(*Rises and stretches out a detaining hand toward* MOE)
Officer.


MOE
(*Stops dialing*)
Doc?


DR. JENNINGS
You know I shot him. You guessed it when I made that slip about the one minute. I had been sitting in this chair just one minute after I obeyed that delightful impulse. I wiped the gun on my coat. It was so simple.


MOE
(*Relieved*)
O.K. So you shot him.


SOPHIE
(*Runs toward doctor*)
Doctor, you didn't, you couldn't have—


DR. JENNINGS
Please, Mrs. Baumer. A jury will find, I hope, extenuating circumstances. I'm sorry, too, that we've played this ugly

170

game so long. But I was so hoping that we'd find some way to pin it on dear Otto—for at least the morning editions.

HORST

Ha! But I'm not a Dummkopf! I foresaw your strategy. The first thing I made you say was, I never moved *after* I came to the radio!

DR. JENNINGS

Yes, that was my error. Now, Officer, let's get going. I'm ready.

(HORST *obligingly goes to open the door for* MOE *and* DR. JENNINGS.)

MOE

But I ain't, Doc. Sit down. (*Presses* DR. JENNINGS *gently into wing chair, and walks toward the center of the room and confronts them all fiercely*) Now let's everybody stop yammering about guns. That's what's been confusing me.

DR. JENNINGS

I don't understand—

MOE

Nobody said anything about a knife. Somebody else stabbed him! (SOPHIE *buries her shocked face on* DENNY's *ever obliging shirt front*) I'm sorry, lady. But holy Jeez, a guy that's been stabbed first don't shoot himself after. And after a guy has been shot he ain't in no shape to tickle himself with a knife. (*Pleased*) That's how I deducted a double murder.

HORST
(*White*)

Stabbed? With what kind of a knife?

MOE

With a cork-handled knife which had some foreign words on it.

MAX

That was yours, Horst!

MOE

(*To* HORST)

Say, you sure travel with an arsenal! Don't happen to have a time bomb on you?

HORST

(*Livid*)

You won't find my fingerprints on that knife! Cork doesn't hold them!

MOE

If you knew that, we'll hold it as evidence against you!

HORST

(*Green*)

How was he stabbed?

MOE

Right through the heart, slantwise over his right shoulder.

HORST

Impossible for me. *I* was born left-handed.

DR. JENNINGS

No doubt you were a left-handed conception.

HORST

(*Purple*)

You've got nothing against me! I have my alibi now. (*By*

172

*the radio*) I was here when they went over to argue with him. Argue—they settled that argument, I'll wager!

SOPHIE

Tom, it isn't worth it!

DENNY

(*Pushing her behind him and confronting* MOE)
Listen, Officer. Baumer *was* already dead when Sophie and I got there—

SOPHIE

(*Hysterically trying to get out front*)
Tom, I just can't stand—

DENNY

(*Shoving her back*)
We saw that he'd been stabbed, murdered. I realized at once that it could be said she or I had done it. I was glad he was dead, so I didn't care a hang if I protected the killer! So I just wiggled him about in the chair, in case anyone was watching us, and pretended he'd said that about the radio when we got back to the sofa—

MOE

But how you gonna prove he was dead?

DENNY

We can't prove it. But we've already proved that Horst was up there *just* before us.

HORST

They can't prove it, because they did it!

173

MOE
(*Incredulous*)
So I'm off the hook now, sweetheart?


HORST
(*Inspired*)
No . . . Finkelstein . . . *You* were the one who said you'd like to run six inches of steel through his swastika!


MOE
Yeah. But this wasn't no kosher killing. (*One hand on* HORST's *heaving bosom*) This was *your* knife, Otto! (*Shoves him roughly away.*)

HORST
Very well. But you and those two lovers had motives. How many times must I say I had no motive!
> (MAX *has been watching* SOPHIE *and* DENNY *with growing alarm. They have been behaving in a very guilty fashion. Throwing all caution to the winds, he now comes to their rescue.*)


MAX
Oh, yes, you had one. Horst, *you* were about to be liquidated!

HORST
(*Gasping*)
That's a lie!

MAX
Baumer told me this afternoon he had a plan to liquidate you.

HORST

(*Squealing with rage*)

You double-crosser!

MAX

You were told to get yourself killed and make it look as though a Jew had done it. Oh, I know the mind of a Nazi!

MOE

(*Commiserating*)

The pleasure is all yours, Baron.

DENNY

He's right! Before the brick came in, Horst was standing there by Hitler. "You're the martyr they want," you said to Baumer, and he said, "You're the martyr they'll get."

SOPHIE

Yes, I remember! And then Horst said: "Yes, I will kill for him!"

MOE

Why'd you say that?

HORST

Oh, just the enthusiasm of the moment. (*Chattering with fear*) You can't prove that Baumer wanted me liquidated!

MAX

Yes. In Baumer's safe are the Berlin papers ordering that liquidation. (*Moves to safe.*)

HORST

You can't touch anything in that safe! Everything in that

safe, in this house, is the property of the German Government!

MOE

(*Stopping* MAX)

He's got me there, I ain't got no right to trample with no murdered man's papers. But I don't need 'em! I've got a motive, an opportunity, and a swell chain of circumstantial evidence pointing directly at Otto!

HORST

(*Rises*)

You've got exactly the same chain of evidence pointing to the Baron!

MOE

(*Grabs* HORST, *shakes him*)

Yeah, and now what was *his* motive?

HORST

(*Shouting*)

The letter! (*To* MAX) That letter Baumer gave you was a letter from London about your grandmother! What can that mean? Why is any Nazi interested in any other Nazi's grandmother? I know the answer to that one! It's classic! And when I came in this afternoon, you had Baumer by the throat! That was about this letter! (*Dashes to fireplace, retrieves half-burnt letter.* MAX *follows him. They struggle for a moment for its possession.* MOE *rushes after them.*)

MOE

Break it up! (*Takes the letter from* HORST *and comes forward with it. He starts to read haltingly*) German? Ihr Vater war ein— (*Pauses*) Jude.

176

MAX

(*Stretches his hand toward the letter. Calmly*)
Let me translate it for you.

MOE

(*Crumpling the letter until his knuckles show white,
then smoothing it out, and pocketing it*)
Jude? I know that word in any language.

MAX

Listen, Officer—

MOE

(*Bitterly*)
I'm listening. Spill it!

MAX

Yes, I wanted to kill him when I first found out about that
letter. But later I only wanted to die myself. Yes, I went to the
desk, but I went there to kill myself—

HORST

So you took the gun and stabbed him! I mean—the knife!

MOE

(*Shouting at* HORST)
O.K., Mr. Goebbels! (*A pause, then wearily*) So where do
we go from here? I'll tell you. Still nowhere. The Baron and
Otto say he was alive. (*To* DENNY) You and Mrs. Baumer say
he was dead. Now all you still gotta do is stick to them
stories. The only thing that's different now is there's two Jews
in it. And still a lot of helpless people four thousand miles

177

away from where we're sitting who are going to take the rap for *both* of us. (*Sits on the sofa at right*) I'm tired. Mr. Denny, will you call the Homicide?

SOPHIE

No, Officer, no!

MOE

Yes, ma'am.

DENNY
(*Steps before* SOPHIE)
Get this quick. I stabbed him!

SOPHIE
(*Calmly*)
He's lying, because I did it.

DENNY

Sophie!

MAX

Oh, Sophie, don't try to shield me any longer!

DENNY

She's not shielding Max. She's shielding me.

SOPHIE

I'm not shielding anybody. It was my murder! I hated him so. But I didn't plan it. The knife was just there— (*Smiling sadly*) It was rather a Nazi inspiration. (*A pause. They know she has spoken the truth.* DENNY *takes her in his arms.*)

**178**

**DENNY**

It's all right, darling. You also had extenuating circumstances.

**MAX**

(*Agonized*)

But she'll be extradited. Tried in a German court.

**DENNY**

No. Tomorrow she'll be the wife of an American citizen.

**MOE**

Well, Father O'Grady's a pal of mine— He's the prison chaplain—

**SOPHIE**

Prison—

**DENNY**

Yes, but I'm an accessory, darling. I'll be there with you—

**MOE**

Gee, lady, I'm sorry. I figured you'd done it.

**SOPHIE**

How?

**MOE**

Women use knives mostly. That's what comes from hanging around the kitchen. I'd like to have let you off this, but I got other women to consider. (*Goes to telephone.*)

**HORST**

Don't forget, you said I could turn her over to the reporters!

179

MOE
(*Appraisingly*)
That's the first thing you said made me think you had guts
enough to commit murder. But yours would be a cold-blooded
murder. (*Lifts receiver.*)

DR. JENNINGS
Officer, just a minute. I'd like to examine the body.

MOE
That's the coroner's job.

DR. JENNINGS
(*Very convincingly*)
But I doubt if a woman has the strength to reach a man's
heart with a knife.

MOE
Doc, you can't fool no coroner. He'd see there ain't no
blood around your wound.

DR. JENNINGS
But I'm sure my bullet did it.

DENNY
(*Reasonably*)
Officer, you've been batting for Mulrooney quite some time,
why not let the Doc bat for the coroner?

MOE
O.K., Doc. Have I been lousing up regulations! (DR. JEN-
NINGS *goes behind the drawn curtains of the alcove*) No

matter how you look at it, murder's gonna be awful embarrassing for His Honor and the Department. (*Dials.*)

MAX

Suppose we'd been able to pin it on Horst, I wonder if we'd've gone through with it.

DENNY

Willingly.

MOE

Nope. In the end, none of you would have done that.

DENNY

Why do you say that?

MOE

To do a thing like that, you gotta be a heel in your heart. (*In phone*) Homicide, please. Captain Mulrooney . . . (*To the others*) I figured if I couldn't make none of you confess, that Otto probably was our party.

HORST

I'm a realist! I'd never have confessed!

MOE

(*In phone*)

Captain Mulrooney? Finkelstein—Post 25 speaking— Yeah, I'm at the Consul's— Yeah— Plenty of trouble— Listen, Captain Mulrooney—he's dead— Listen, Mulrooney, he was murdered— (*Holding his hand over receiver to duck the blast that is coming out of it*) Mulrooney's embarrassed. (*Into*

*phone*) Yeah, I got the guy who done it— Yeah— O.K.—
Captain. (*Hangs up*) The squad'll be here in five minutes.

HORST

So you're a Jew, Baron? That explains why you never
liked me.

DENNY

That's one possible explanation for it.
> (MOE *takes out his police notebook and pencil and be-*
> *gins to catch up with the proceedings.*)

MAX

I have the same eyes, the same fair hair, quite the same
face I had this morning. But now, because I had a grandmother I never laid eyes on, I'm no longer a Nazi—not even
a German. Officer—

MOE

(*Cheerfully*)

Call me Moe, Max.

MAX

Moe—if I am the same as I was this morning, what are the
Jewish things about me now?

MOE

They'll say all the bad things. Soon you'll say it's all the
good ones.

MAX

I suppose I'll get used to it.

MOE

Nope, you'll never get used to it—

MAX

(*Rebellious*)

Moe, why are we so different?

MOE

So we're a race of extremities. It's surprising. We go the whole hog from guys like Gyp the Blood and Lepke to guys like Einstein and Eddie Cantor.

MAX

But Moe— (*Bitterly*) You don't know what I've done to my own people.

MOE

Listen, Max—Jews and Christians is alike in one thing. They're always persecuting their brothers.

MAX

What would Hitler say if he found out his mother was Jewish?

MOE

He'd say he was Jesus.

MAX

I have a lot to do when I get back to Berlin.

SOPHIE

Oh, Max, you can't go back. You know what they'll do to you.

MAX

If I can't stand it, I'll know what to do, Sophie. Sometimes death's the only way for Germans like me to stay in their beloved country. If I were not what I am, I'd like to be an

American. (*Smiling at* DENNY) I see now that makes a lovely difference.

HORST

Not so much. You'll spend the rest of your life in a concentration camp; they'll spend theirs in prison.

DR. JENNINGS

(*Comes from alcove in a state of great excitement*) Officer! Officer! Mrs. Baumer's knife did *not* kill him!

SOPHIE

Dear Doctor—I'm not afraid for myself any more.

DR. JENNINGS

Neither am I, for myself. Now listen carefully. We've got to work fast. I examined him. He'd been drinking—

MOE

Jeez, Doc, don't tell me he died of delirious tremens!

DR. JENNINGS

He was poisoned! Cyanide potassium!

MOE

Jeez! It's a massacre!

DR. JENNINGS

He was quite dead when Mrs. Baumer got to him. He drank it from a glass on his desk. (MOE *moves toward alcove quietly*) No, I haven't touched it.

184

**HORST**

Poisoned! So that still leaves you, Baron!

**MAX**

(*Eagerly*)

And you, Horst. Now I'm fighting and I like it—in the open.

**MOE**

Doc, tell me what you can tell me.

**DR. JENNINGS**

Cyanide drains all oxygen from the blood instantly. It is over in less than a minute. But he must have had spasms, short but very ugly spasms. Now, if he drank after he sat in that chair, he would have fallen out of it. It is safe to assume that he drank while he was on his feet—and fell into it!

**MOE**

Listen, he had them spasms while you all thought he was opening the windows—

**DENNY**

Then whoever put the poison in his glass did it *before* he went to the desk?

**DR. JENNINGS**

Most certainly.

**HORST**

This puts everybody right back in the picture!

**MOE**

Aw, nuts! It ain't reasonable that the Doc here poisoned

him an hour before, and then, having gotten away with that, shot him. The same thing goes for Mrs. Baumer.

HORST

One or both of them may have been trying to confuse the issue.

MOE

All those in favor of granting that the Doc and Mrs. Baumer only did one murder apiece raise his right hand and signify by saying "Aye."

ALL BUT HORST

Aye!

HORST

No.

MOE

Overruled!

HORST

No!

MOE

We got a democratic majority. So that leaves Mr. Denny, Max and you, Otto.

DENNY

Horst, is my heart in this one!

MOE

*(Uneasily)*

But when you got poison, you usually got a premeditated murderer. Them kind don't never confess.

186

SOPHIE

But, Officer, the poison was perfectly available. It was in the right-hand drawer of the desk.

MOE

How do you know that, lady?

SOPHIE

I found it in his medicine chest this morning. I accused him of poisoning Mr. Churchill with it two hours ago.

HORST
*(Things are coming too fast for him now)*
Mr. Churchill?

MOE

A mere detail, Otto. Go on, lady.

SOPHIE

Max and I saw him put it in the drawer. I mean—I don't know about Max, but I saw him.

HORST
*(Triumphantly)*
Max! She's sold you up the river with that slip!

DR. JENNINGS

Nonsense. I knew it was there too.

DENNY

So did I. Sophie told me.

187

MOE

Anybody here who didn't know that desk was the chamber
of horrors?

HORST

I didn't.

MOE

Doc, is the poison there now?

MAX

No, it isn't. Moe, I told you I went to that desk. I went
there to find the poison, but it was gone—

HORST

Stop! If the poison's not in the drawer, where is it? It must
be on someone's person. I demand to be searched!

DENNY

Don't be a damned fool!

MOE

Otto, you go off on more scents than a plastered blood-
hound.

HORST

I demand it!

MOE

(*Grabs* HORST *violently and efficiently begins to un-
button him, as over his shoulder he says to* DENNY
*and* DR. JENNINGS)

O.K. You asked for it. You two democrats can search each
other.

188

DR. JENNINGS
(*Whispering to* DENNY)
Crime quickly becomes a habit. The safe was open, so I've relieved the German Government of Horst's records. (*Takes out* HORST's *reports and puts them into* DENNY's *pockets*) Spy reports, maybe. (*To* MOE, *loudly*) Denny's are empty! (DENNY *starts to search* DR. JENNINGS.)

SOPHIE
(*To* MAX)
Think where Horst was when Karl got his drink.

MAX
(*Listlessly feeling through his own pockets*)
I know the answer to that one. Nowhere near Baumer.

DENNY
(*Suddenly takes out a big package of bills from* DR. JENNING's *pocket*)
What's *this?*

DR. JENNINGS
(*Whispering*)
Fifty thousand dollars in Nazi funds. To buy myself assorted political refugees. (*Looking at* SOPHIE) One in particular from Czechoslovakia.

DENNY
(*Puts money back in* DR. JENNINGS' *pocket and slaps him on back. To* MOE, *loudly*)
The doctor's are empty!

189

MOE

(*He now has* HORST's *uniform unbuttoned, thrust back from his shoulders, so that* HORST *is considerably tangled up in his own belts and buckles*)

Momma would love this. Hey, what's this? (*He fishes out a number of small bank books and a roll of bills from* HORST's *inner breast pocket*) Bank books . . . and *more* bank books . . . And a bank roll.

DENNY

Moe, I'd keep those. So many banks. An income-tax evader.

HORST

(*Reaches for them*)

Give me those! They're my property!

MOE

(*Opening* HORST's *shirt to disclose a shiny metal bullet-proof vest. He taps it. It emits a hollow tinny sound*)

Anybody got a can-opener?

MAX

(*Reaches into his own pocket and finds the bottle of poison. He glares at it for a moment while* SOPHIE *looks at him, petrified*)

What's this?

MOE

(*Comes toward* MAX *and takes the poison away from him*)

The poison.

SOPHIE

(*Horrified*)

Max!

HORST
(*Triumphant*)

Dummkopf!

MAX
(*Staring helplessly at* MOE)

Moe, I didn't!

MOE
(*Gently*)

I *know* you didn't. You wouldn't poison no guy and then sit around like a dumb cluck for two hours hatching the evidence in your pocket.

HORST

Why wouldn't he?

MOE

On account of the brains he inherited from his grandmother!

HORST

Then how did the poison get in his pocket? I suppose I planted it?

DENNY

That's a damned good suggestion. If we can find out when you did it!

MOE

Look, folks. We gotta go back to where Baumer got that drink!

DENNY

That was just before the brick came through the window—

MOE

O.K. Everybody back to where the brick was flang through

the window. (*They all take the now already familiar positions. Then wearily*) If I get canned from the force, I can always get a job as a movie director.


DR. JENNINGS
(*Sitting*)
I was sitting in this chair—


MOE
You was sitting in that chair and you'd have saved a hell of a lot of time if you'd never got out of it. O.K. Where's the Consul when he gets his drink?


DENNY
There at the bar. (*At fireplace*) I'm here.
(MOE *goes to bar.*)


SOPHIE
(*Near* MAX)
I was here.

HORST
I had already poured myself a beer. I was here— (*In corner*) quite remote from human contact.


MAX
(*In easy chair*)
I didn't even go to the bar. I was here.


MOE
O.K. I'm the Consul. Now what?

MAX

You pour me a whiskey. Then you pour yourself your own brandy. (MOE *pours two drinks as told by* MAX.)

DR. JENNINGS
(*Suddenly rising*)

His own *brandy?*

SOPHIE

He never drank anything but brandy—

DENNY

A taste acquired in the tropics—

MAX

Yes. He said something about the House of Rothschild . . .

DR. JENNINGS
(*Going to him*)

Max! He poured himself a brandy?

MAX

Yes. Oh, I never touched his glass. He poured both his and mine.

DR. JENNINGS
(*Grabbing* MOE)

Officer, stop! The solution of any crime lies in the personality of the murdered man.

MOE
(*Agonized*)

Doc, whatta ya got?

DR. JENNINGS

This one lies in the Consul's tropically acquired taste for brandy. Because the glass (*Pointing to alcove*) in there is *whiskey*.

MOE

Doc, you don't mean— (*Goes to table, smells* MAX's *glass, and looks up, the dawn of a great good light on his face*) So help me God, *this* is straight brandy! (*To* MAX) You had the letter on you. The poison in your pocket—

DENNY

Which Baumer slipped in when, Max? Think, man!

MAX

(*Rising, with sudden happy remembrance*)

When—when he came to console me—to put his arms around me—here.

SOPHIE

Oh, Max, darling! He told me he knew you were going to commit suicide!

HORST

(*Consistent to the last*)

But it's quite obvious he didn't!

SOPHIE

Oh, don't you see, you nitwit! My husband staged Max's suicide!

HORST

(*With heavy satire*)

And at the last minute he changed his mind and took the poison himself?

MAX

(*Shouts*)

No! The brick!

ALL

The brick?

MAX

(*Falls into the easy chair, moaning with mirth*)
The brick changed it for him!

MOE

Now wait a minute! (*Takes* HORST's *beer and* MAX's *brandy from the small table to bar. Returns with two glasses he poured at bar. Shouting*) O.K. I'm the Consul. (*To* MAX) Here is your whiskey. (*Puts one glass on table*) This is my brandy. (*Toasts the bust with the other glass*) Heil Pickle-puss! Whang! Bang! Brick!

DENNY

Confusion! And you call for the policeman—

MAX

Then you set the brandy on the table. (MOE *does so.*)

SOPHIE

For one fraction of a second—

DR. JENNINGS

And then you pick it up again— (MOE *picks up other glass.*)

MOE

(*Almost reverently*)
And it's a glass of poisoned whiskey!

195

MAX

(*Ecstatic*)

Oh, put it on his tombstone! The Third Reich allows no margin for error!

(*There is the swift clamor of the police sirens and motorcycles rounding the corner again.*)

HORST

(*Disgusted as he looks toward the alcove*)

Well, the Dummkopf! (*Making one last try*) But you can't prove that Baumer switched those glasses accidentally before the reporters get here!

MOE

Listen, boys. How we gonna prove it definitely so this schmutz can't possibly smear it?

DR. JENNINGS

Listen! I was sitting in that chair—

MOE

You're telling me!

DR. JENNINGS

—when the brick sailed in. Naturally I turned. I saw Baumer set his brandy down. Then—I attached no significance to it at the time—I quite definitely saw him pick up Max's whiskey!

SOPHIE

Why, I did too! I very definitely recall it!

DENNY

Why, hell, so did I see that!

196

MAX

So did I.

HORST

But I didn't!

MOE

Now, Otto, who's gonna take your word against the word of a couple of Jewish boys in this city? (*The sirens give way to the clanging of the police wagon outside*) That's the pie-wagon.

SOPHIE

But, Officer! The doctor and I did stab and shoot him.

DR. JENNINGS

Mrs. Baumer, there are no penalties attached to such delicate attentions to a corpse.

DENNY

You are murderers emotionally, but not legally.

MOE

Yeah. But das Otto is headed for der Clink. (*With a swift, happy, practiced gesture he puts handcuffs on* HORST.)

HORST

Handcuffs? On me? Why, I'm the only one in this room who didn't try to murder the Consul—

DENNY

Maybe that's an offense in itself, Otto.

197

HORST
*(Struggling)*
You can't hold me on anything!


MOE
Carrying concealed weapons—pending income-tax charges.
(*Showing* HORST *to the door*) What'd you say your lawyer's
name is?

HORST
Ouch— Benjamin Rosenblatt.


MOE
If he gets you off this, you oughta make him an honorary
Aryan.
> (*The door bursts open and* CAPTAIN MULROONEY *enters.
> He is six feet of powerful, red-faced, exasperated
> authority.*)

MULROONEY
*(Bellowing)*
Now, Finkelstein, what the hell's happened!


MOE
*(Sheepishly)*
Well, Captain Mulrooney, it seems the Consul was shot,
stabbed and poisoned.

MULROONEY
Well, the son of a bitch— Did it kill him?


*Curtain*

CPSIA information can be obtained
at www.ICGtesting.com
Printed in the USA
BVHW051124080223
658118BV00022B/341